# JEWISH PRAYER: CONCEPTS AND CUSTOMS

*Jewish Prayer: Concepts and Customs*
is a part of
**The Hebraica/Judaica Bookshelf**
edited by
Yehiel Hayon

Alpha Publishing Company
is a division of
Special Edition, Inc.
Columbus, Ohio

# JEWISH PRAYER: CONCEPTS AND CUSTOMS

By

Earl Klein

Alpha Publishing Company
Columbus, Ohio
1986

All rights reserved.

Copyright © 1986 by Earl Klein.

No part of this book may be reproduced, stored in a retrieval system, or transmitted, in any form or by any means—electronic, mechanical, photocopying, recording, or otherwise—without the prior written permission of the publisher.

**Library of Congress Cataloging in Publication Data**
Klein, Earl, 1925–
Jewish prayer.
(The Hebraica/Judaica bookshelf.)
Includes bibliography and index.

1. Prayer (Judaism). 2. Siddur. 3. Judaism—Liturgy. I. Title. II. Series.
BM669.K59     1986     296.7'2     85-23944

ISBN 0-933771-01-0

# Permissions

The author wishes to thank the following for permission to use excerpts from the copyrighted material indicated.

Abraham Joshua Heschel, *Man's Quest for God.* Copyright, 1954, Abraham Joshua Heschel; copyright renewed ©, 1982, Hannah Susannah Heschel & Sylvia Heschel. Reprinted with permission of Charles Scribner's Sons.

*Sefer ha-Ikkarim* by Joseph Albo, translated by Isaac Husik. The material is copyrighted by and used through the courtesy of The Jewish Publication Society.

Reprinted by permission of Schocken Books Inc., from *The Kuzari* by Judah Halevi, Hirschfeld translation. Copyright ©, 1964, by Schocken Books Inc. All rights reserved.

The Soncino Press Limited, excerpts from *Horeb* by Samson Raphael Hirsch, translation by I. Grunfeld, 1962 edition. All rights reserved by the Soncino Press Limited.

Reprinted with permission of Macmillan Publishing Company from *The Yeshiva*, Part II, by Chaim Grade, translated by Curt Leviant. Copyright ©, 1972, Chaim Grade.

Reprinted with permission of Dover Publication, Inc., from Moses Maimonides, *The Guide for the Perplexed,* translated by M. Friedlander, second edition.

Reprinted with permission from *Literature of the Synagogue* by Joseph Heinemann and Jakob Petuchowski, 1975 edition. Published by Behrman House Inc., 1281 Broadway, New York, New York 10001.

B'nai B'rith International, from Moses Mendelsohn, *Selections from His Writings,* edited by Eva Jospe. 1975 edition.

To my dear wife, Snira

It is proper before commencing one's prayers to recite the following: "I hereby take upon myself the obligation of performing the positive commandment, 'And you shall love your fellowman as yourself.'"

> Prayerbook of Rabbi Isaac Luria, the Ari,
> 16th century.
> Rabbi Abraham Gombiner, Commentary Magen Avraham on Orach Chayim 46:1,
> 17th century.

To worship God and do good unto man are the purpose and goal of our existence; they represent our destiny in this life and our hope for the next. All else is insignificant.

> Moses Mendelsohn, letter, 1782.

# TABLE OF CONTENTS

|  |  |
|---|---|
| Preface | xi |
| 1. The Philosophy of Prayer | 1 |
| 2. Prayer as a *Mitzva* | 13 |
| 3. Structure and Composition of Prayers | 17 |
| 4. *Kavana* and Frame of Mind | 24 |
| 5. Time, Place, and Community | 29 |
| 6. Preliminary Blessings | 38 |
| 7. *Pesukei de-Zimra*—Verses of Song | 46 |
| 8. *Keri'at Shema*—The *Shema* and Its Benedictions | 53 |
| 9. The *Amida* | 73 |
| 10. Manner and Mode of Prayer | 95 |
| 11. Dress and Ceremonial Accouterments | 104 |
| 12. Benedictions *(Berachot)* | 122 |
| 13. The *Kaddish* | 129 |
| 14. The Torah Service | 136 |
| Notes | 144 |
| Selected Bibliography | 172 |
| Index | 175 |

# PREFACE

PRAYER IS ESSENTIAL to the life of the Jew. He refuses to exist without it. Judah Halevi said in *The Kuzari:* "Prayer is for his soul what nourishment is for his body. The blessing of one prayer lasts till the time of the next, just as the strength derived from the morning meal lasts till supper." Of all his spiritual activity, prayer occupies more of the average Jew's time than any other.

Two desiderata pervade the devotion to prayer. One is the need of the Jew for communion with the Almighty—a wish to elevate oneself above the mundane. The other is the urge for fellowship with other Jews in the synagogue—a means of dispelling feelings of isolation in an alien world. In biblical times, prayer was spontaneous and individual. It was tailored to respond to particular events, perhaps a cry for help in time of trouble, or an expression of praise and thanksgiving in time of gladness. Later prayer evolved into a community activity with more structured recitations.

By the time of the Men of the Great Assembly (458-202 BCE), the prayer service became formalized with specific selections to be recited in an established order. From that core, the prayer service developed into what it is today. Interestingly, the number of prayers periodically increased, but rarely, if ever, suffered deletion.

In ancient times, some of the prayers existed only in outline form. There was a formula, but no fixed verbatim content. With the advent of the printed prayerbook, the selections became standardized. Even before the printing press, Jews must have shown signs of concern with the worship service, because one rabbi in the time of the Mishna warned against making one's prayers fixed and routine (M Avot 2:18). At least since that time, Jews have concerned themselves with the twin requirements of a meaningful service: *keva* and *kavana*—fixed prayer and inner devotion.

I am a *davener* and always have been. As such, I too have faced the predicament of the praying Jew: How does one maintain interest in and derive inspiration from a structured, repetitious worship service? My response was not to be overcome by a sense of futility. Instead I resolved to search out ways to make my participation in the age-old services more meaningful. I started on a program of study to learn about the origins of the prayers, the reasons for their inclusion in the service, and the related laws, customs and concepts.

My research began in earnest while I was teaching a Talmud class at Sinai Temple in Los Angeles. The materials included Tractate Berachot, which deals with prayers and blessings. From there I moved on to other sources and texts. I began to jot down notes, and eventually I accumulated an extensive card file of references. I found that, as Jewish tradition teaches, familiarity breeds affection; that study of Torah leads to love of Torah. I gained new insight and interest. The prayer services acquired for me added inspiration. It was as the Psalmist said, "a new song" (Ps. 96:1).

I decided after a time to share what I had learned. In the following pages, my purpose has been to discuss the structure of the prayer services, the customs associated with them, and the underlying religious and philosophical concepts. In every instance, I have attempted to make known the source and rationale of the rituals. In lawyerly fashion, I have attempted to cite for the reader the most appropriate authority known to me.

The subject of Jewish prayer is so fertile and exciting that a full exposition of all of the materials dealing with rites and customs of the numerous Jewish communities and movements would fill volumes. The material is virtually inexhaustible. To make this work manageable, I have necessarily concentrated on the daily, traditional, Ashkenazic service. Mention of other rites is limited to occasions where it was necessary to show contrast or to illustrate a particular point.

"From all of my teachers have I gained knowledge" (Ps. 119:99). Most of the information came from study of texts. However, from time to time, I have discussed various topics with friends and acquaintances. The ones to whom I am indebted are too numerous to mention. I thank them all. I do wish, however, to express specific thanks to Sinai Temple (Los Angeles), University of Judaism, and Yeshiva University of Los Angeles, whose libraries I used regularly, and to their library staffs for their courtesies. I acknowledge specially the assistance of my wife, Snira, who is a faculty member of the University of Judaism and of the Sinai Temple Hebrew School. She advised me on Hebrew language questions and gave me the benefit of her academic knowledge on numerous subjects. I also wish to thank my daughter, Peninna, who showed great interest in my work and explored prayer ideas with me.

Los Angeles E. K.
November 1985

# 1.
# THE PHILOSOPHY OF PRAYER

IN THE PAGAN WORLD, the origins of prayer were magic and incantation; the worshiper attempted to combat evil spirits and powers or influence the deities by spells or conjurations. Although there may have been elements of incantation in the worship of some Jewish sects, biblical and mainstream Judaism were free of those influences.[1] In later Judaism, the emphasis was on communication with the Almighty. Stress was placed on the influence of prayer on the individual worshiper, not its impact on God.

When one thinks of worship, one usually thinks of the English word *prayer*, which denotes a request or supplication. In Jewish tradition, Divine worship encompasses much more. The major categories are: *bakasha* and *techina*—supplication; *toda*—thanksgiving; *vidui*—confession; *beracha*— benediction; *limud*—study; *edut*—affirmation; and *tehila*—praise.

A long history of persecution and of personal deprivation has caused Jews, collectively and individually, to place particular emphasis on worship as a pouring out of the heart and a crying for help. Numerous biblical expressions point to such dependence. For example: "Give ear to my words, O Lord, consider my meditation. Hearken unto the voice of my cry, my King and my God, for unto Thee do I pray" (Ps. 5:2-3); "Hear the voice of my supplications, when I cry unto Thee" (Ps. 28:2). In the Talmud,[2] one finds the report that King Hezekiah said to the prophet Isaiah, "This tradition I have from the house of my ancestor: 'Even if a sharp sword rests upon a man's neck, he should not desist from prayer.' "

What is the purpose of prayer? What is its special meaning to the Jew? An oft-quoted statement of William James declares that man prays because he must. The apparent meaning is that man has a need to pour out his heart, in joy and in sorrow, in confession and in thanksgiving. James' statement perceives prayer as a subjective need of man, as a means of ventilation of inner emotion. In it there is no ostensible specific requisite of a relationship with a higher being.

The Jewish concept of prayer presupposes the participation or the involvement of the Almighty. The questions previously posed, as they relate to the traditional Jew, concern God's role in the prayers of man, the effect of man's prayer on God, and the effect of man's prayer on man. Prayer is defined in Jewish tradition as "service of the heart." It is a *mitzva*, a commandment, according to Maimonides.[3] Prayer is therefore a concern of God. It is regular and continuous contact with the Almighty. As Jewish tradition sees it, man is enabled at fixed times every day to raise his sights and contemplate God and the spiritual life.

Maimonides said in *The Guide for the Perplexed*:

> We must bear in mind that all such religious acts as . . . praying . . . serve exclusively as the means of causing us to occupy and fill our mind with the precepts of God, and free it from worldly business; for we are thus, as it were, in communication with God and undisturbed by any other thing.[4]

Judah Halevi said in *The Kuzari*:

> Prayer is for his [the Jew's] soul what nourishment is for his body. The blessing of one prayer lasts till the time of

the next, just as the strength derived from the morning meal lasts till supper. The further his soul is removed from the time of prayer, the more it is darkened by coming in contact with worldly matters.[5]

Abraham J. Heschel has stated:

Moral dedications, acts of worship, intellectual pursuits are means in the art of sanctification of time.... Acts of worship counteract the trivialization of existence. Both involve the person, and give him a sense of living in ultimate relationships. Both of them are ways of teaching man how to stand alone and not be alone, of teaching man that God is a refuge, not a security.[6]

Prayer gives man the opportunity to pour out his being to God, to express his humility and his dependence on Him, and to give thanks for His bounties. Prayer is not only a means of approach to God, it is actual communication with Him. The Psalmist wrote: "In my distress I called unto the Lord, and He answered me" (Ps. 120:1); "I will lift up my eyes unto the mountains. From whence shall my help come? My help comes from the Lord" (Ps. 121:1-2). But prayer is not only communication in times of distress, it is also expression of praise and thanksgiving in times of joy. Once again the Psalmist best captures the worshiper's thoughts:

It is a good thing to give thanks unto the Lord
and to sing praises unto Thy Name, O Most High;
to declare Thy lovingkindness in the morning,
and Thy faithfulness every night (Ps. 92:1-3).

Heschel's approach to prayer includes another concept, which touches on the mystical. He says that prayer is "the opening of our thoughts to God;" it is

our humble answer to the inconceivable surprise of living. God is in search of man, and prayer clears the path for God's approach. The purpose of prayer is to be brought to God's attention, to be listened to, to be understood by God; not to know Him, but to be known to Him.[7]

Prayer is also a time for introspection and confession. It has often been explained that the foremost Hebrew term for the verb *to pray* is *lehitpalel*, which is the reflexive form of the verb meaning "to judge." Thus, to the Jew, "to pray" means "to judge oneself."[8]

Samson Raphael Hirsch, in his *Nineteen Letters,* says: "All the various component parts of the Hebrew worship subserve this great purpose, the bringing of man into communication with [God]."[9]

He explains elsewhere that the key to Jewish prayer is not in petitions to God, nor in experiencing religious emotion, but in honest self-scrutiny before God and in confronting the great truths of the Torah. He further states that prayer means "stepping out of active life in order to attempt to gain a true judgment about oneself, that is, about one's ego, about one's relationship to God and the world, and of God and the world to oneself." Prayer, he says, strives to infuse the mind and the heart with the power of such judgment as will direct both anew to active life, purified, subliminated, and strengthened.[10]

He goes on to explain that the aim of prayer is purification, enlightenment, and uplifting of our inner selves, as well as the cleansing of thought and heart.[11]

Maimonides in the *Guide* states that repentance and confession are important elements of prayer. Man, he says, who is not free of sin or error, by confessing his errors, studies his behavior, repents, improves himself, and strives to become better than he was.[12]

Prayer also provides a time for affirming one's belief in God and for expressing allegiance to God and His Torah. Some of the basic portions of the worship service are declarations and affirmations of certain truths. Foremost of those is the *Shema,* which declares the Unity of God. The Jew in that sense uses prayer as a means of reviewing the articles of his faith and of pledging allegiance to those principles.

Hirsch says that prayer is not mere petition and not mere ecstasy of devotion and adoration. A proper idea of prayer, he urges, includes "the possession and expression of proper conceptions and resolutions concerning our own personality and our duties toward God, the world and mankind."[13]

Referring to the *Shema,* Chief Rabbi Hertz stated:

> It is a proclamation of the existence and Unity of God; of Israel's complete loyalty to God and His commandments; the belief in Divine Justice; the remembrance of the liberation from Egypt, and its corollary, the Election of Israel. These are foundation pillars of the Jewish Faith.[14]

Some of the other declarations of faith are *Ani Ma'amin, Yigdal,* and *Emet ve-Yatziv.* Study also plays an important part in the worship of the Jew. Portions of the service include passages from the Bible, the Mishna, and talmudic literature. That those passages are a part of the prayerbook confirms that for the Jew worship is a study experience.[15] Hirsch points out that among Jews, synagogues are called *shuls* or schools, because the reading of the Torah imparts instruction and wisdom.[16]

## Prayer as Petition

Philosophically there has always been a problem about that facet of prayer dealing with petition and supplication. The specific issues needing resolution are these: Does the individual have the right to make demands on God? Does God answer prayers? Does He change the course of events in response to man's prayers? A non-Jewish clergyman once summed up the above questions in this way: "Is God a divine bellhop, operating a heavenly room service for those who sound the buzzer?"

One Jewish writer expressed the issue as follows:

> Can we hope to alter by our prayers what God has already preordained? ... [It] is pertinent to point out that it would be surely near to blasphemy to think of God as automatically granting the requests of all-comers. If every time we prayed for something our prayers were granted, the act of praying would cease to be a demonstration of faith, but would descend to a sort of formula of incantation.[17]

Another writer expressed a similar thought that if all prayers were answered favorably, prayer would not be an act of worship, a demonstration of faith, nor a desire for communion with God, and "synagogue attendance would degenerate into a system of incantation in which thaumaturgy had replaced devotion."[18]

The impact of prayer on the natural course of events is not treated extensively in the Talmud. In one of the few places, the Mishna in Berachot states:

> ... to cry over the past is to utter a vain prayer. If a man's wife is pregnant and he says [God] grant that my wife bear a male child, this is a vain prayer. If he is coming home from a journey and he hears cries of distress in the town and says [God] grant that this is not my house, this is a vain prayer.[19]

In explanation, the Talmud and Rashi indicate that once an event has occurred or has become fixed, prayer cannot avail.[20]

The 15th-century philosopher Joseph Albo in *Sefer ha-Ikarim,* The Book of Principles, treats the subject at length. Preliminarily, he states that

> every one who believes in Providence must believe that prayer will help him and save him from misfortune. If one does not pray in a time of trouble, it is either because he does not believe in Providence, or ... he doubts God's ability to save him, ... or ... he doubts whether he is worthy of the privilege of having his prayer heard.[21]

Albo says that those who doubt the efficacy of prayer argue as follows:

> Either God has decreed that a given person shall receive a given benefit, or He has not so determined. If He has determined, there is no need of prayer; and if He has not determined, how can prayer avail to change God's will that He should now determine to benefit the person, when He had not so determined before?[22]

But prayer does avail, according to Albo. He explains as follows:

1. *Prayer changes a person.* Repentance benefits a wicked man, for through repentance, he becomes

another person, as it were, concerning whom no such evil decree was made.

> If you set your heart to pray and to improve your conduct, there is no doubt that through prayer and right conduct you will escape from these troubles. From this it is clear that prayer and right conduct are always helpful in nullifying a divine decree. Our rabbis also say: "The cry [of prayer] is good for a man both before the divine decree and after."[23]

As for the objection that the Divine will cannot be changed by prayer, the answer is that the Divine will in the first place is that the decree should be realized if the person in question continues in the same state, and that the decree should be changed if the person's state changes.[24]

2. *Petitioning God for our needs shows our dependence on Him.*

> [Prayer] service consists in mentioning God's praises, acknowledging that all things come from Him, requesting God to supply our needs in supplicating Him and acknowledging that we have no other helper and support outside of Him.[25]

3. *Prayers are not answered at times because God is unwilling.* Albo says:

> All the acts which a man does do not necessarily realize the purpose intended in doing them. It happens that a person does all that is necessary in the proper way and yet fails to realize the purpose intended. . . . So in the case of prayer. It often happens that a person prays in a proper way, at the proper time, and yet his prayer is not accepted . . . because the will of God does not assent.[26]

Albo explains that one reason prayer may not be accepted is that "God knows that the favor requested is not good for the supplicant, and hence his prayer is not accepted by way of providence for his own good. . . ." Albo suggests that man leave the discretion in God's hands whether to answer prayer and that he couch his prayers with that thought in mind.[27]

He says:

> The best kind of prayer is therefore that of the wise man, who said: "O Lord, do Thy will in heaven above, show kindness to those who fear Thee here below, and do what is good in Thine eyes." . . . Then he says: "And do what is good in Thine eyes," that is, whatever it is that I pray to Thee for, attend not to my words or request, to do what my heart desires, or what I ask, for many times I ask and pray for something which is bad for me, thinking it is good. But Thou knowest better than I whether the thing is good for me or bad. Therefore decide Thou and not I; do what Thou knowest is good.[28]

**4. *Man should not push too hard in his demands*.** Albo suggests that although man should petition God for his needs to show his dependence on Him, he should not be too demanding but place his fate in God's hands.

> [The] most fitting prayer is to ask the divine favor in general terms and not in terms definite and specific. A person who prays to God in particular and specific terms is, as it were, desirous of forcing the divine will to his own ideas and preferences instead of bending his ideas to God's will; but this is tantamount to a contempt for God's knowledge and power, as though God knew no other way of granting his request except the one which he [man] has chosen.[29]

Summarized, Albo's teachings demonstrate that prayer in the first instance changes man, not God; that the purpose of prayers of petition is to show man's dependence on the Almighty, rather than to seek a concrete response; and that the petition should not be for a specific answer but for whatever God in His discretion and wisdom believes is good for man.

In modern times, Hirsch also voices a similar approach, that the purpose of prayer was to influence man. Pointing to the Talmud's definition of prayer as *avoda she-ba-lev* ("service of the heart"), Hirsch explained that prayer was the "inner service" which prepared man for his struggles in the outer world. As previously mentioned, he observed that the verb *lehitpalel*, commonly translated as "to pray," originally meant to deliver an opinion about oneself, to judge oneself.

He states:

> In other words, [prayer is] an attempt to gain a true judgment of oneself.... In tefillah you gather the strength of dedication for life, allowing this life to become the fulfillment of the Divine will, the furthering of the Divine purpose—a contribution to the success of that purpose, which God has set for humanity and Israel. Thus the flower of all tefillah is the resolution which infuses the whole man and unites all your powers to be a servant of God in life.[30]

In the *Nineteen Letters,* Hirsch states that the aim of worship is purification, enlightenment, and uplifting of one's inner self to the recognition of the Most High and one's duties towards Him; not mere stirring up of the emotions, empty sentimentalism, and unreasoning tears, but the cleansing of thought and heart.

He says further:

> Life robs us of the correct judgment concerning God, the world, man and Israel, and concerning our own relation to them. Leaving the disturbing influences of life and turning to God, you can approach and find Him in the mystic contemplations of tefillah. All of the various component parts of the Hebrew worship subserve this great purpose, the bringing of man into communication with Him, who is concealed from view in his [man's] daily life.[31]

In discussing prayers of petition and supplication, Hirsch states that they represent man's humble petition that God may continue His bounty to him, and express man's humble appeals to His unfailing mercy to heal his weaknesses and backslidings.[32]

A more contemporary thinker, Heschel, also is critical of stressing self-interest in worship. He says that in prayer "we shift the center of living from self-consciousness to self-surrender," and that

> [prayer] takes the mind out of the narrowness of self-interest and enables us to see the world in the mirror of the holy. For when we betake ourselves to the extreme opposite of the ego, we can behold a situation from the aspect of God. Prayer is a way to master what is inferior in us, to discern between the signal and the trivial,

between the vital and the futile.... Prayer clarifies our hope and intentions. It helps us discover our true aspirations.... It is an act of self-purification, quarantine for the soul.[33]

Further, Heschel says: "The focus of prayer is not the self.... It is the momentary disregard of our personal concerns, the absence of all self-centered thoughts, which constitute the art of prayer."[34]

## Prayer as Praise and Blessing

Other aspects of Jewish worship that raise philosophical questions are the prayers of praise *(tehilot)* and the formula of the benediction *(beracha)*. That formula is usually translated as "Blessed art Thou," etc. Addressing what is conceived as a problem, some modern editors translate the formula as "Praised art Thou." The problem is how can man have the temerity to "bless" or "praise" Almighty God. The first difficulty is that God has no need of man's blessing.[35] Secondly, it is usually the lesser personality who looks to a superior for praise and blessing.

In one response, Louis Jacobs states that the benedictions are in a sense symbolic. The purpose of the blessings cannot be to fill a need of God, he says, but rather to direct the minds of men to higher ideals.[36] Jacob Emden (1697-1776) in his commentary on the prayers, *Siddur Beit Ya'akov,* states that *baruch* ("blessed") is not a passive past participle, but a noun like *rachum* ("merciful"). Thus he translates *baruch* to mean that God is the source of blessings.

Another way of resolving the matter is to trace the meaning of the word *beracha.* Its derivation is the word *berech* ("knee"), and its original source was probably *bereicha* ("well"), where one kneeled to drink water. Taken in that context, *beracha* means not an expression of arrogance, but a statement of obeisance and respect.

In a similar vein, Hirsch states that benedictions supply man with the firm resolution to promote the fulfillment of the Divine will in the midst of life, so busy with transitory cares and devoted so much to material aims. He thus concludes that whenever you say to God "Blessed art Thou" you are subjecting all of your powers to the fulfillment of His will and dedicate yourself to His service by the blessing and the concurrent deed.[37]

## Some Questionable Concepts

Three other ideas about prayer deserve mention. Those are primarily prayer notions of non-observant persons, who may express doubt about the familiar concepts of God, or who may question whether He listens to prayer.

One concept is that prayer is a matter of tradition. A person may not believe in the efficacy of prayer, but he may acknowledge that prayer is part of Jewish tradition. While he may not believe in a theological purpose for prayer, he prays because as a matter of tradition, Jews pray. Heschel calls this "religious behaviorism." He states:

> As a personal attitude, religious behaviorism usually reflects a widely held theology in which the supreme article of faith is respect for tradition. People are urged to observe rituals or to attend services out of deference to what has come down to us from our ancestors.[38]

He contends that such a doctrine lacks spontaneity and is not concerned with the inner life.

A second idea is that prayer helps one identify with the Jewish people. Heschel refers to this as "prayer as a social act." He criticizes it as an approach "built on a theology which regards God as a symbol of social action, as an epitome of the ideals of the group." Although he agrees that identification with the people of Israel is important, Heschel argues that the identification is important only to the extent that it emphasizes "Israel's unique association with the will of God." Otherwise one is dealing with mere nationalism.[39]

The third concept is that prayer serves a useful purpose for the individual. Those following that view reason that, although there may not be a God Who hears prayer, spending a few hours in prayer is good for one's psyche or well-being. Heschel calls this "religious solipsism." He criticizes the doctrine as maintaining that the self of the worshiper is the whole sphere of prayerlife and that one should pray because "prayer is a useful activity" and "is good for one's health."[40]

Louis Jacobs responds to Heschel with the assertion that although those reasons for prayer may be inadequate in themselves, they can provide supplementary reasons for the value of prayer. He says:

> Jewish prayer does provide the Jew with a powerful means of identifying himself with his people and with its past. And the idea of praying to the good in ourselves is not entirely unknown in the traditional Jewish sources.[41]

It might be added that the above discussion considers prayer in the abstract, in theory. As a practical matter, anyone who enters a synagogue for the purpose of praying has some inner involvement with the idea of a providential God, no matter how slight. Moreover, it is a key concept of Jewish tradition, that one who performs a *mitzva* without the proper intent or purpose is to be encouraged, for he may eventually perform it for the proper reasons.[42] One may never learn the proper purpose of Jewish prayer unless one starts somewhere.

## 2.
## PRAYER AS A MITZVA

MAIMONIDES CONSIDERED PRAYER as a biblical commandment. In the *Mishneh Torah*, he says:

It is a positive commandment to pray each day, as it is said: "And you shall serve the Lord, your God (Exod. 23:25)." From tradition, they learn that service means prayer, as it is said: "And to serve Him with all your heart" (Deut. 11:13). The Sages said: "What is service of the heart? It is prayer."[1]

He numbers prayer as fifth in his list of 613 commandments. He points out that, although prayer is a command of the Torah, the times and details are supplied by the Rabbis.[2]

Nachmanides (1194-1268), however, considered prayer as a command of the Rabbis. He interpreted Deuteronomy 11:13 to refer to worship in general, but not specifically to prayer, or the *Amida*. He explained that one of the merciful attributes of the Creator is that He hears and responds whenever we call upon Him, but specific prayer is not a Torah command, except prayer in time of trouble. Nachmanides interpreted Deuteronomy 11:13 to command man in general terms that all of his service of God be wholehearted.[3]

## The Prayer Services

The Men of the Great Synagogue (458–202 BCE) instituted the three daily statutory prayer services: morning *(Shacharit)*, afternoon *(Mincha)*, and evening *(Ma'ariv* or *Arvit)*. In addition to those basic services, there were supplementary services on special occasions. Examples were the Additional Service *(Musaf)* to be recited whenever there was an additional sacrifice; Welcoming the Sabbath *(Kabalat Shabbat)* on Friday eve, and Conclusion *(Ne'ila)* at the end of Yom Kippur.

The Talmud[4] attempts to trace the origins of the three basic services. One view was that they were instituted by the patriarchs:

> Abraham established the morning service, as it says: "And Abraham got up early in the morning to the place where he stood" (Gen. 19:27), and "standing" means only prayer.... Isaac instituted the afternoon prayer, as it says: "And Isaac went out to meditate in the field at eventide" (Gen. 24:6), and "meditation" means only prayer.... Jacob instituted the evening service, as it says: "And he lighted upon the place" (Gen. 28:11), and that means only prayer.

Some trace the origin of the Yiddish word *davenen* ("prayer") to that theory. The Aramaic word for "from the fathers" is *da-avonan.*[5]

Another view[6] traced the three services to the sacrificial order. With the destruction of the Temple, prayer was substituted for the offerings. A classic reference was from Hosea 14:3, "And we shall render for bullocks, the offering of our lips." Another was from Psalms 141:2, "May my prayer be set forth before Thee as incense...."

According to that view, the morning service represented the morning sacrifice, the *Tamid;* and the afternoon prayer, the afternoon sacrifice, the *Mincha.* There was no evening offering, but the Rabbis found sanction in the fact that portions of the sacrifices not consumed by evening could be burned all night.[7] The indirect authority for the evening service led to a contention that it was optional.[8] The view that the evening prayer was mandatory (at least at the decree of the Rabbis) eventually was accepted.[9] The basis for the additional service is clear. An *Amida* was added on those days when a mandatory additional sacrifice was brought in Temple times in observance of a particular occasion.[10] Although prayer was often compared to the sacrifices and was often mentioned as a substitute, the Talmud states that prayer was more important than the sacrifices.[11] A midrash makes the same point. Song of Songs Rabba on verse 5:2 states: "I am sleeping—from sacrifice, but my heart is awake—for prayer. I am sleeping—for the Temple, but my heart is awake—for the synagogue and study house."[12]

## Three Services

A question had been raised whether one should pray continuously, if one assumed that prayer was a praiseworthy act. The response was that constant, continued prayer would be trifling with the Almighty and would dilute the efficacy of prayer.[13]

The Rabbis settled on the concept of three prayer services. Precedent was found in tradition.[14] David prayed three times a day and stated: "As for me, I will call upon God, and the Lord will save me. Evening and morning and at noonday, will I complain, and moan, and He hath heard my voice" (Ps. 55:17-18). Daniel also offered prayer three times a day: "And he kneeled upon his knees, three times a day, and prayed and gave thanks before his God" (Dan. 6:11).

The idea of three prayer services daily has been attributed to Moses as well. The Midrash states that Moses foresaw a time when the Temple would be destroyed and offerings would cease. He thereupon instructed Israel to pray three times each day.[15] Three services spread throughout the day served the important purpose of focusing man's attention on God and spiritual matters during his waking hours.

It has frequently been asked whether set services at set times do not destroy spontaneity. Some have argued that one should pray whenever one has the urge, as was done in biblical times, and thus make supplication to the Almighty more spirited. The classic statement of Israel Abrahams was: "What can be done at any time and in any manner is apt to be done at no time and in no manner."[16]

# 3.

# STRUCTURE AND COMPOSITION OF PRAYERS

## Length of Prayer

A frequent topic of rabbinical debate was whether long or short prayers were more acceptable. Some Rabbis expressed concern that if one were to spend too much time at prayer, he would have no time to study Torah or earn a livelihood.[1] Another concern was that a man who prayed all day might call on the Almighty thoughtlessly.[2]

One disciple, while leading the prayers, expanded them greatly. When complaints were made to Rabbi Eliezer, he replied that Moses prayed forty days and forty nights (Deut. 9:18,25). On another occasion a certain disciple shortened the prayers. When complaint was made to Rabbi Eliezer, he responded, again referring to Moses: "Is he any more concise than our master, Moses, who prayed, 'Heal her now, O God. I pray Thee,' and Miriam was healed" (Num. 12:13).[3] Finally Rabbi Eliezer summed it all up and said: "There is a time to be brief in prayer, and a time to be lengthy."[4]

Whether prayer was to be long or short, the Rabbis frowned upon prolongation of praises of God with numerous adjectives. The Talmud [5] tells of a reader who, while leading the prayers, said: "O God, the great, mighty, terrible, majestic, powerful, awful, strong, fearless, sure and honored." Rabbi Chanina waited until he had finished and said: "Have you concluded all the praises of God? Even the three that we do say in the *Amida*'s first paragraph 'great, mighty and terrible,' had not Moses mentioned them in the Torah (Deut. 10:17) and had not the Men of the Great Synagogue inserted them in the *Tefila*, we should not have been able to mention them." The Rabbi then explained that mortals can never adequately exhaust the recitations of all of God's praises. To recite a portion is therefore an insult.

Jews were directed to adhere to the format of prayers established by the Rabbis. The Men of the Great Synagogue instituted for Israel blessings and prayers, sanctifications and *havdalot*.[6] Jews were admonished not to vary the formulas *(matbea,* or mintage) of benedictions and prayers.[7] Certain of the prayers were not fixed verbatim. In early times, the general content and the concluding benediction were fixed.[8] The prayer forms became more standardized after the invention of the printing press and as prayerbooks became available to worshipers. Even today there are significant differences in the specific wording of some prayers in the Ashkenazic and Sefardic rites.

## *Formulas*

The formulas created by the Rabbis were to assist the average person in fulfilling the obligation of prayer. Not every person is articulate; not every man can easily express in words the thoughts that are in his heart. George F. Moore[9] said that the rabbinical forms of prayer furnished the common man "with simple and appropriate language to express what in his simplicity he would have found no words for."

Using established words of prayer, the individual was certain to express deep religious feeling as well as keep the well-being of the community in mind. Critics have complained that they prefer "spontaneous" words of prayer, but very few have the ability to compose words with the depth of meaning and beauty of expression as did the Rabbis of old. One who hopes for spontaneity and instantaneous inspiration may have a long wait. When special moments of inspiration do arrive, the worshiper is encouraged to include those private prayers at the close of the *Amida.*[10] The opportunity for spontaneity is not stifled by use of the rabbinic forms.[11]

Abraham J. Heschel has stated that a fixed pattern of liturgy does not impair the element of inwardness or self-expression because to pray, one needs both empathy and expression.[12]

One of the characters in Chaim Grade's great novel, *The Yeshiva,* says:

> There are those who don't understand how a man can recite the same prayers all of his life. The worldly people maintain that even a poet who sings his own songs must continually produce new ones. Those who don't pray themselves can't imagine that when a Jew recites a psalm with all his heart, the ancient poem becomes the worshiper's own brand-new poem, just as all of creation is made new daily for the man of faith. Every sensitive man has a day in his life when he awakes and looks at the sun as if he had never seen it before. Of course no one dreams that a new sun would actually materialize before his eyes. Similarly, new prayers aren't necessary for the person who prays with all his heart and soul.[13]

## *Language*

In addition to format, language of Jewish prayer has always been a source of discussion and debate. The question usually is "Why Hebrew?" Prayer need not be exclusively in Hebrew, although it is preferred and is the norm. For example, the Mishna in Sota[14] provides that the following may be recited in any language: the

*Shema,* the *Tefila (Amida),* and the benedictions over food. On the other hand, the following must be recited in Hebrew: the paragraph of the first fruits (Deut. 26:3,5-10), the words of *chalitza,* the blessings and the curses (Deut. 27:15-26), the benediction of the priests, and the benediction of the high priest on Yom Kippur. One interpretation of the verse *Shema Yisra'el* ("Hear, O Israel") states that the *Shema* may be recited in any language that is familiar to the worshiper.[15] Legend maintains that the ministering angels carry one's prayers to the Almighty. Rav Judah and Rav Jochanan therefore cautioned against prayer in Aramaic since the angels understood Hebrew only.[16] Some rabbis permitted use of languages other than Hebrew when prayer was with the congregation, but insisted on Hebrew only for solo prayer.[17] Others disagreed. Mishna Berura[18] states that a community needs no intermediary and therefore can pray in any language. There was another concept mentioned in the Talmud, although not necessarily tied in with prayer, that although secular matters may be uttered in Hebrew, sacred matters must not be uttered in a secular language.[19]

The modern practice of traditional congregations is to recite almost all congregational prayers in Hebrew, except for those old, established prayers said in Aramaic. Some recite selected prayers in the common language of the country.

Hebrew has always remained the preferred language of Jewish prayer. Some of the reasons are:

1. *Judaism is a universal religion.* Jews are a universal people. A unique language links Jews, wherever they may reside and whatever language they may use in daily conversation. Prayer in Hebrew permits a Jew to pray with his fellow Jews from any other country. Jews are thus one people bound together, with a single religious purpose, expressed in a common language.

2. *Hebrew is the unique language Jews use to express their special relationship to God.* Language is not a mere code of interchangeable signals. Language repre-

sents not only words but thoughts and feelings as well. Hebrew expresses the thoughts and feelings of the Jew. A translation can try, but will never completely succeed. Such words as *chesed, rachamim,* and *shalom,* may be translated as "lovingkindness," "mercy," and "peace," respectively, but translation will never convey their true meaning. A Jew must articulate his prayers in the Hebrew language, which expresses his full thought and emotion.

3. *One purpose of Jewish worship is to educate the Jew.* Requiring prayer in Hebrew encourages study of the language. The common complaint that one cannot understand Hebrew must be answered with the advice to study Hebrew. Once that is accomplished, the Jew is capable of studying and understanding the Bible and other Jewish classics. A whole new experience is open to him.

## Music

Music has always been closely associated with Jewish worship. Throughout the Bible, there is mention of spontaneous music, vocal and instrumental, as a means of praising God. Some examples are the Song of Moses (Exod. 15:1, *et seq.*), the victorious returns from battle of Jephtah, David, and Saul (Judg. 11:34; 1 Sam. 18:6-7), and the transporting of the Ark (1 Chron. 13:8, 15:16).

During the periods of the Temples, organized music was a part of the services. The Levites were instructed to furnish song for the sacrificial rites.[20] They sang songs in the Temple, morning and evening, accompanied by instruments (1 Chron. 23:30, 16:8; Neh. 12:27-29,34). There was also an orchestra of Levites (1 Chron. 25:7).

Certain prayers were recited and rituals performed to the accompaniment of song. The offering of the first fruits featured the sound of the flute.[21] Rabbi Meir stated that singing preceded the sacrifice of the burnt offering.[22] The congregation recited hallelujahs to song.[23]

Interpreting the verse, *lishmoa el ha-rina* (1 Kgs. 8:28), the Talmud recommended that prayer be recited in a joyous setting and with song.[24]

Rabbi Jochanan stated that if one reads Scripture without a melody or repeats a mishna without a tune, of him it is said: "Wherefore I gave them also statutes that were not good" (Ezek. 20:25).[25] Just as study requires a tune as an aid to memory, so does prayer. In time there developed a series of melodies adapted to the prayer services. Each service developed a chanting or musical mode or style of its own, known as *nusach*. Some communities created their own *nusach* for each prayer.

Music at the worship service serves five basic purposes:

1. It beautifies the service. A beautiful sound is one of three things that restore a man's good spirits, according to the Talmud.[26]
2. It is an aid to memory and makes it easier to learn and remember the prayers.
3. Music is a source of inspiration, enthusiasm, and joy. A non-Jewish source once said that "he who sings at prayer, prays twice."
4. Music is a means of introducing change in the highly formalized prayers. The statutory prayers may not be altered as to content, but by varying the tunes, new attitudes and interest can be fostered. Abraham Milgrom describes music as an "antidote to the routinization of prayer."[27]
5. Music calms a person and puts him in a proper frame of mind for prayer. William Congreve said: "Music hath charms to soothe a savage breast."[28]

## *The Cantor*

Closely associated with the musical aspects of the service is the cantor. In Hebrew, he is called *chazan*, which is derived from the Aramaic *chazana*, meaning superintendent or officer. The *chazan* originally had charge of the synagogue premises and its contents.[29] On Erev Shabbat he gave the trumpet signal to cease work. He brought the Torah scroll into the synagogue or temple for reading[30] and sometimes led the prayers.[31] Because of the nature of his duties, he became familiar with the prayers and the music. Eventually in the geonic period, he took over the function of leading the prayer service.

The general designation for the prayer leader is *sheliach tzibur*—messenger of the community. The Talmud[32] states that the leader of prayers should be one who is experienced, whose house is empty (meaning either poor or sinless), whose youth was spent decently, who is modest and agreeable to the people, who knows how to chant and has a sweet voice, and is well versed in Jewish lore and prayers. Rashi on the above passage states that only one acquainted with the melody and with a pleasant voice should recite prayers before the congregation.[33]

In the Ashkenazic ritual, the cantor is a prayer leader. He chants the first words of a prayer and concludes by reading the last few verses. In the Sefardic ritual, the prayer reader recites each and every word of the prayers aloud. In that sense, he prays for the congregation. The custom is also reminiscent of the period before prayerbooks were available to each worshiper.

## Musical Instruments

With the destruction of the Temples, the Rabbis forbade the playing of musical instruments during the prayer service, as a sign of mourning. That rule is still observed in Orthodox synagogues, where the only instrument permitted is the *shofar*. Its use is not strictly for musical purposes, but for the express purpose of fulfilling a *mitzva*, and therefore does not fall under the ban.

# 4.

# KAVANA AND FRAME OF MIND

PRAYER IS COMMUNICATION with the Almighty. The Rabbis saw it as an event requiring special preparation. They were concerned about attitude and proper frame of mind; one was to pray in a reverent manner.[1] Rabbi Eliezer ben Hyrcanus told his disciples: "When you pray, know before Whom you stand."[2] Although his statement referred in particular to the *Amida*, it was appropriate to all worship.

The Jew was instructed to pray only in a proper and respectful frame of mind; he was not to pray when in a mood of sorrow, indolence, or frivolity, while engaged in laughter or idle talk, nor immediately after litigating a case, nor after discussing a halachic matter.[3] From the story of Hannah (1 Sam. 1:12-15) it was deduced, among other things, that one was forbidden to pray while drunk.[4] Not only was it disrespectful, but drunkenness interfered with *kavana*.

Prayer was to be recited in calmness of spirit, in a mood of rejoicing over the performance of a *mitzva*. The

Talmud[5] stated that one who prayed should tarry and meditate one hour before prayer and one hour after, as did the early pious ones. Rav said[6] that one whose mind was not quieted should not pray, and Rabbi Chanina would not pray when irritated. A traveler who was frightened of probable attack by highwaymen was instructed to offer a short prayer[7] rather than attempt to compose himself and recite the complete service. Maimonides said:

> If one finds that his mind is confused and his heart is troubled, it is forbidden for him to pray until he has become composed. Therefore one who has come from a trip and is fatigued or is worried, it is forbidden for him to pray until he has become quieted.[8]

The worshiper, once in a proper state of mind, was required to avoid distractions. Others were warned against walking within four cubits of one who was reciting the *Amida*.[9] One of the reasons for covering the head with the *talit* during prayer was to eliminate distraction. Praying while facing a wall served the same purpose.[10]

In addition to approaching prayer in a proper state of mind, the worshiper was enjoined to pray with *kavana*. The term is derived from the Hebrew word *kivun*, meaning direction. *Kavana* is variously translated as directing the mind, intent, concentration, or devotion. The Talmud states that he who prays should direct his heart heavenward.[11]

The rabbinical debate over *kavana* at prayer was part of a more comprehensive discussion whether *mitzvot* in general must be performed with intention. A man was compelled by force to eat *matza* on Passover. A man blew the *shofar* simply to make music. He was reading the passage of the *Shema* in the Torah, and the time for reading the *Shema* arrived. In each of the foregoing cases, the question was whether he performed the respective *mitzva*. Some authorities took the position that no *mitzva* was performed unless there was intent. Others argued that doing the act was all that was required, regardless of intent.[12] The debate worked its way throughout talmudic and later rabbinic lore. The general statements about the need for *kavana* had special nuances dependent upon the kind of *mitzva* and the context in which an act was performed. For example: If one put on *tefilin* at the time of the morning prayer, it was evident that his intent was to perform a *mitzva*. If he picked up his *lulav* and *etrog* during the festival of Sukkot during the day, his act could be ambiguous. He might be moving them from one place to another, or he might be taking them for the purpose of performing a *mitzva*.[13]

Maimonides appears to take inconsistent positions. Regarding *matza*, he says that if one eats without intent, he has fulfilled his obligation.[14] About the *shofar* he says that unless the one who blows the *shofar* and the one who listens both have the intent to fulfill the *mitzva*, the listener has not fulfilled his obligation.[15] The commentaries, in an effort to resolve the inconsistency, say that Maimonides is of the opinion that *mitzvot* require intent, but in the case of *matza*, the person had a general intent, i.e., he knew he was eating and that it was Passover night.[16]

Rabbenu Jonah (13th century) offered the opinion that whatever the rule concerning a *mitzva* requiring an express act, there is a difference where the *mitzva* consists only of reciting words. *Kavana* is necessary in that case because, if the worshiper has no *kavana* and performs no act but merely recites words, it may appear that he is doing nothing.[17]

Just as *kavana* may be translated in various ways, it has various definitions as to legal and religious effect. It can mean the mere intention to perform an act, which is known in common law as "general intent." That would exclude an act done accidentally. It can also mean the intention to perform an act in order to bring about a particular result, i.e., to perform a *mitzva*, known in law as "specific intent." It was the latter kind of *kavana* that engaged the Rabbis in their discussions. *Kavana* also has a special connotation in prayer—praying with concentration on the meaning of the words.[18] Mishna Berura[19] discusses *kavana* as being of two types: (1) *kavana* of the heart, i.e., concentration on the *mitzva*—in prayer that would mean attention to the meaning of the words; and (2) *kavana*, intent, to fulfill a particular *mitzva* by performance of an act. It is mentioned that even among those authorities who hold that *mitzvot* do not require *kavana*, a competing or counter-intent will invalidate the act.

With reference to the reading of the *Shema*, the Rabbis established that at least the first sentence, *Shema Yisra'el*, must be recited with the intent to declare God's Unity and to accept the yoke of the Kingdom of Heaven. Rabbi Akiba insisted that the entire reading required *kavana*.[20] Maimonides ruled that "one who reads the *Shema* and does not direct his heart at the first verse—which is 'Hear O Israel'—has not fulfilled his duty; as for the remainder [of the *Shema*], if he has not directed his heart, he has fulfilled [his duty]."[21]

The Mishna Berura states[22] that the expression "directing the heart" at the first verse refers to the meaning of the words, but one must also have intent to fulfill the *mitzva* throughout the entire reading of the *Shema*. It was noted that some held the opinion that the intent to fulfill the *mitzva* refers only to the first verse. Maimonides described *kavana* for the *Amida* as follows: One should clear his heart of all thoughts and see himself as though he were standing in God's presence. Therefore he should sit a while before prayer so as to direct his heart.[23]

With further reference to the *Amida*, Maimonides stated[24] that the entire prayer should be recited with *kavana*, but if the first benediction (*Avot*) were recited with intent, the entire *Amida* need not be repeated.

One means of assuring proper *kavana* upon performance of *mitzvot* was the recitation of special preliminary formulas. Those formulas (for example, "Behold I am about to fulfill the commandment of . . .") were objected to by some authorities, such as the Gaon of

Wilna and Ezekiel Landau, as being halachically incorrect or unnecessary.[25] The formulas had their origin in kabbalistic lore, which gave still another meaning to the word *kavana*. There it meant special mystical intentions attached to the words or acts, one being the intent to fulfill the commandment "for the sake of uniting the Holy One, praised be He and His *Shechina.*"[26] Today formulas of that type are recited primarily by Chasidim.

On the subject of *kavana*, the *Shulchan Aruch* recommends a little prayer with *kavana*, rather than much without it.[27] Judah Halevi, speaking of the prayers of a pious man, wrote[28] that his tongue agrees with the thought; he does not speak in prayer in a mechanical way, but every word is uttered thoughtfully and attentively.

Bachya said that "prayer without the heart [devotion] was like a body without a spirit."[29]

# 5.

# PLACE, TIME, AND COMMUNITY

TIME AND PLACE are concepts that pervade all of Jewish religion and observance. Performance of *mitzvot* is usually subject to constraints of particular time frames and locations. Since the destruction of the Temple, place is a more flexible condition of observance, but in ancient times, sacrificial offerings, for example, were restricted to the Temple and to specific areas there. There were also detailed time periods during which particular offerings could be brought.[1]

Those constraints have carried over to the prayer services, which are considered a substitute for the offerings.[2] The rules on time are more exacting than those of place in the post-Temple era. Today, the concern is not the specific location, but the type of place.

## *Place*

The synagogue is the preferred place for prayer. The Talmud states that "a man's prayer is heard by God only in the synagogue."[3] The Rabbis said moreover that God is to be found in the synagogue where a *minyan* prays, and that daily attendance at communal prayers in the synagogue was considered an act that would prolong life.[4] Resh Lakish said that whosoever has a synagogue in his town and does not go there to pray is called an evil neighbor.[5]

If one cannot pray in the synagogue, he should recite his prayers in any clean or appropriate place. A midrash on Psalm 4 states: "When you pray, pray in the synagogue of your town. But if you are prevented from praying in the synagogue, pray in the fields; and if you cannot pray in the fields, pray at home."[6] Thus, the Rabbis sanctioned prayer on the road,[7] atop trees,[8] in the fields,[9] or while riding an animal.[10] One may not pray in a place of filth or excrement, nor in a bathhouse, toilet, or garbage dump. One may not pray near a place of bad odors, corpses, or in view of nakedness.[11]

According to Rabbi Jose ben Chanina, a man should pray in a lowly place, rather than an elevated place, based on the verse, "From the depths I called Thee..." (Ps. 130:1).[12] Following that rule, it became a custom that the prayer leader would conduct the service from a lower place at the front of the synagogue and not from a *bima.*[13] Many synagogues were constructed so that the worshipers walked downstairs to the place of prayer.

It was also a custom of pious persons to face a wall when they prayed. This practice was based on a talmudic reference[14] that King Hezekiah turned his face to the wall and prayed (Isa. 38:2). Maimonides stressed this rule because it aided in concentration.[15] Another ancient rule still followed by many was that laid down by R. Chiya bar Abba, who said in the name of R. Jochanan: "A man should not pray except in a room which has windows, since it says, referring to Daniel, 'Now his windows were open in his upper chamber towards Jerusalem'" (Dan. 6:11). Rashi stated that windows cause a man to direct his heart; he views the heavens and his heart becomes humble.[16] Based thereon, it was a custom to have windows in the synagogue sanctuary.[17] The *Zohar* said that a synagogue requires twelve windows.[18]

The Rabbis also urged worshipers to pray in a fixed place, referring to Abraham.[19] It was also stated that if a man had a fixed and permanent place for prayer, his enemies would succumb to him.[20] A fixed place referred not only to a specific synagogue, but to a specific seat in that synagogue, or at home.[21] When praying, worshipers were instructed to face Jerusalem and the Holy of Holies, when reciting the *Amida*. The Talmud explained that "in this way all Israel will be turning their hearts toward one place."[22] In the synagogue, of course, one must face the Ark.

## Time

Time limitations are carefully observed even today for reasons relating to the sacrificial system as well as to the various divisions of the day, week, month, and season.

As previously mentioned, the prayer services are linked to the sacrificial system and adapt to the time schedule of the offerings. The time for reading the *Shema* is specifically deduced from the Torah itself, which states, "when you lie down and when you rise up" (Deut. 6:7).

### Computation of Hours

In computing the hours, which will be discussed in relationship to the times of prayer, the Rabbis did not refer to the usual 60-minute hour. They calculated the time according to *sha'ot zemaniyot*, seasonal or variable hours, which depend upon the length of daytime during a particular season of the year.[23]

The seasonal hour is calculated as follows: The number of minutes from the start of day until night (sunset) is totaled and divided by twelve hours. The result will be the length of the hour in minutes to be used for computing prayer times. When daytime is twelve hours, the seasonal hour will equal the usual or fixed 60-minute hour. In winter, the seasonal hour will be shorter, and in summer, it will be longer. It should be noted further that there is a variant based upon the definition of the term *start* of day. The Magen Avraham computed the start of day from dawn or the appearance of the first morning twilight. The Gaon of Wilna computed the start of day from sunrise, i.e., when the "face of the East" is lit up.[24]

## Specific Prayers

*Morning Service (Shacharit)*—There are different time periods for the *Shema* and the *Amida*. The time for the morning *Shema* is from dawn or sunrise to the end of the third hour of the day. If one recites the *Shema* thereafter, he has not fulfilled the precise *mitzva* of "Reading of the *Shema*," but is considered as though he were reading from the Torah.[25] The proper time for the *Amida* is from dawn or sunrise until the end of the fourth hour of the day. The Mishna speaks of a time limit of mid-day, and cites R. Judah's deadline of the fourth hour.

*Additional Service (Musaf)*—On days when there was an added offering in Temple times, worshipers today add an additional *Amida*. Those days, for example, are New Moon, Sabbath, and holidays. The time for recitation is after the Morning Service and until the end of the seventh hour, preferably, but it may be said until sunset.[26]

*Afternoon Service (Mincha)*—This service corresponds to the afternoon sacrifice. It may be recited commencing one-half hour after noon. When daylight saving time is in effect, the starting time will be an hour later, always one-half hour after noon by the sun. The outer limit is evening.

There are three types of *Mincha* time periods. The period from one-half hour after noon (six and one-half hours after dawn or sunrise) until evening (twelve hours after dawn or sunrise) is called *Mincha Gedola*, the Great *Mincha*. The period from nine and one-half hours after dawn or sunrise until the twelfth hour is called *Mincha Ketana*, the Small *Mincha*. The latter time was the usual one for the afternoon sacrifice in Temple times. A third period is called *Pelag Mincha*, or Half *Mincha*. That period is derived by dividing the period of the smaller *Mincha* in two: one-half from nine and one-half hours of the day until ten and three-fourths hours (roughly from 3:30 PM to 4:45 PM); and one-half from ten and three-fourths hours until twelve hours (roughly from 4:45 PM to 6:00 PM). *Pelag Mincha* usually denotes the one-and-one-fourth-hour period before evening.[27]

*Evening Service (Ma'ariv or Arvit)*—At this service there is, again, a distinction as to time for the *Shema* and the *Amida*. The time for the evening *Shema* is from the appearance of three stars until dawn.[28] It is the custom in some communities to recite the Evening Service before dark to take advantage of the presence of a *minyan*. In that case, the *Shema* must be repeated after three stars appear.[29] The evening *Amida* is the subject of an interesting discussion. There was no evening sacrificial offering; consequently, there was a talmudic debate whether the evening *Amida* was mandatory or optional.[30] The authority for mandatory recital was that certain parts of the sacrifices offered during the day remained on the altar during the night. But even according to the view that the evening *Amida* was mandatory, there were no definite time limits.[31]

Therefore, the Evening Service may be recited before nightfall, particularly if prayer at that time ensured a *minyan*, and could be said until dawn. By rabbinical decree, recitation of the Evening Service was made mandatory. As a concession to the view that it is optional, the *Amida* is not repeated as at other services, and no *Kedusha* is added.

### Makeup

One who accidentally misses the time period for recitation of a particular *Amida* (except *Musaf*) may "make it up" by reciting two *Amida* prayers at the next prayer service. The second *Amida* must be the same as the one recited in a timely manner should there be any change in ritual. For example, if one misses the afternoon service on Friday, he would be required to pray two Sabbath *Amida* prayers at the Evening Service.[32]

## Community and Individual Prayer

An indispensable feature of Jewish prayer is its link to the community. It is manifested in two ways: Prayers are phrased in the plural, and worship with the congregation is stressed. The image of a pious person isolating himself as he meditates about his own concerns is alien to Jewish worship.

### The Phrasing of Prayers

All statutory prayers are composed in the plural, even those dealing with individual needs. Prayers in the singular, limited to special personal requests, are supplementary and secondary to the basic prayers. When a Jew prays, he does not ask for his needs alone, but for those of his fellowmen as well. Thus, in the *Amida*, he asks forgiveness by saying, "Forgive us, O our Father, for we have sinned . . . ," and beseeches God for healing, by saying, "Heal us, O Lord, and we shall be healed. . . ."[33]

The Talmud[34] tells of a dispute whether one should petition for his personal needs before or after recitation of the prayer for the community. The final decision was that one should first pray for the needs of the community and then for himself. Private supplications may be inserted at particular places in the *Amida*, or at the conclusion.[35] Private prayers were encouraged in the blessings "Who hears prayers" *(shomea tefila);* "Heal us"; and "For prosperous years"; or after "Who blesses His people with peace."[36] Abayei said that one must always include the community in his prayers.[37] One must always pray for others, and failure to do so is considered sinful.[38] Even a solitary traveler in a dangerous area is instructed to offer a short prayer, and that prayer is not for selfish ends, but was formulated as follows: "Save, O Lord, Thy people, the remnant of Israel; in every time of crisis may their requirements not be lost sight of by Thee. Blessed art Thou, O Lord, Who hearkens to prayer."[39] An 18th-century rabbi summed it up as follows: "A prayer not spoken in the name of Israel is no prayer."[40]

Community prayers are discussed by Judah Halevi in *The Kuzari.* He expresses the view of the Talmud that "a prayer in order to be heard must be recited for a multitude." Thereafter Halevi's rabbi explains to the king the advantages of common prayer, e.g., a community will never pray for a thing that is hurtful to an individual; and common prayer is worthier because it profits the whole world. If each individual prays for all others, the deficiencies of any individual's prayers will be corrected by the prayers of others.[41] The rabbi explains: "A person who prays but for himself is like him who retires alone into his house, refusing to assist his fellow-citizens in the repair of their walls."[42]

## Public Prayer

Although statutory prayers may be recited in private, prayer with the congregation is preferred and emphasized in Jewish life. The Talmud[43] states that one who has a synagogue in his city and does not attend is called a bad neighbor and brings exile upon himself and his children. Interpreting the verse from Psalms 69:14, "May my prayer unto Thee, O Lord, be in an acceptable time," the Talmud states that "an acceptable time" is when the congregation prays.[44] Therefore, although the

Rabbis encouraged prayer in the synagogue, if one could not attend, he was to recite his prayers in private at the time the congregation worshiped.[45]

The *Sifrei* advises that God does not reject the prayer of the multitude.[46] Another reason for public prayer given by the Talmud was that there was song and rejoicing where the congregation gathered. On the verse, "to hear the song and the prayer" (1 Kgs. 8:28), the Rabbis commented that prayer is to be recited where there is song.[47]

Joseph Hertz stated that the Jewish prayer service was conceived as primarily congregational in that the worshiper prays not as an individual but as a member of a brotherhood.[48] Abraham J. Heschel said that private prayer will not survive unless it is inspired by public prayer; the way of the recluse, exclusive concern with personal salvation, and piety in isolation from the community are acts of impiety. He expressed the thought in this way: "The Jew does not stand alone before God, it is as a member of the community that he stands before God."[49]

In the prayerbook of Isaac Luria (16th century), the following preliminary statement is found: "I hereby take upon myself the obligation of performing the positive commandment, 'And you shall love your fellowman as yourself' " (Lev. 19:18). Luria suggested that the statement be recited before commencing one's prayers.[50]

## The Minyan

The basic prayers as already mentioned may be recited in private. Certain prayers may be recited only in the presence of a *minyan*—a quorum of ten males, all at least thirteen years and one day old. That the *minyan* should consist of ten was arrived at according to the Talmud as follows:

> Rabin bar R. Adda says in the name of R. Isaac: How do you know that the Holy One, Blessed be He, is to be found

in the synagogue? For it is said: "God stands in the congregation of God" (Ps. 82:1).[51]

Rashi there explains that "congregation" *(eda)* means ten by reference to the story of the twelve spies in Numbers 14:27, where God complains: "How long shall I bear with this evil congregation *(eda)*," which excluded Joshua and Caleb, and thus consisted of the remaining ten.[52]

A *minyan* is required for certain prayers and ceremonies, where the prayer or event constitutes a special sanctification of God. *Kedusha* (sanctification upon repetition of the *Amida*) and *Kaddish* (mourner's prayer) are examples of such special prayers. The Torah may be read only in the presence of a *minyan*. The reason is derived from the verse, "I will be sanctified among the children of Israel" (Lev. 22:32). The Rabbis commented thereon that "for any manifestation of sanctification not less than ten are required."[53]

# 6.

# PRELIMINARY BLESSINGS

THE INVOLVEMENT OF THE JEW in prayer and ritual commences from the moment he awakens. He is governed by two well-known maxims: "One should strengthen oneself like a lion to arise in the morning to worship his Creator,"[1] and "I have placed the Lord before me always" (Ps. 16:8). Thus, as soon as he arises from his bed, he must wash his hands and recite a benediction. When he performs his bodily needs, he recites a second blessing.[2]

The benedictions are mentioned in the Talmud.[3] The benediction for washing the hands is "Praised art Thou . . ., Who has sanctified us by Thy commandments and commanded us on the washing of the hands (*netilat yadayim*)." The Mishna Berura[4] gives various reasons for washing the hands on arising: (1) Upon awakening a person is like a newborn creature and must sanctify himself. (2) One's hands may have become soiled by touching parts of the body during the night and must be cleansed. (3) Upon awakening for the new day, one must prepare for the service of God, just as the priests did, when they washed their hands before commencing their service each day in the Temple. The Torah states: "And Aaron and his sons shall wash their hands... when they go into the tent of meeting... or when they come near to the altar to minister..." (Exod. 30:19-20).[5] The water must be poured over the hands from a vessel, using *koach gavra* ("human force"), just as the priests did.[6] The benediction does not literally mention washing. One authority derives the word *netila* from *natla*, a cup used for holding water, with which to wash the hands.[7] Another view is that *netila* is derived from the word *natal*, meaning "to take" or "lift." Thus, the blessing refers to lifting the hands after washing.[8] The blessing has been associated with the words of Psalm 134:2, "Lift up your hands in holiness" *(Se'u yedeichem kodesh)*. Samson Raphael Hirsch in his *siddur*[9] explains that the hands are lifted from physical endeavor to a higher purpose as one starts the day. The sense is that one dedicates his activity for the day to God's service.

This is one instance where the benediction is recited *after* performance of the *mitzva*.[10] The reason is that one's hands may not be clean before washing, and a blessing is inappropriate when one is in an unclean state. The benediction "Who has formed man in wisdom" *(asher yatzar)* is thereafter recited, whether one has attended to his bodily needs or not.

Those two benedictions are followed in most prayer services by two blessings concerning the study of Torah. There is a debate in the Talmud[11] as to which benediction should be recited over the *mitzva* of Torah study. Rabbi Judah said in the name of Samuel that the proper blessing is: "Praised... Who sanctified us... and commanded us to study the Torah." Rabbi Jochanan used to conclude: "Make pleasant... the words of Thy Torah in our mouth." Rav Hamnuna said the blessing should be: "Praised... Who hast chosen us from all the nations and has given us the Torah. Praised... Who has given us the Torah." After discussion, the Rabbis concluded that all of the blessings had merit and suggested that all be recited. Tosafot mentions[12] that utterance of the Torah blessing in the morning suffices for the whole day, and refers to a French custom of reciting some sections of Scripture and the Oral Law, i.e., the Priestly Benediction (Num. 6:24-26) and *Eilu Devarim* (a mishna in Tractate Pe'a, chapter 1, and a baraita from Tractate Shabbat 127) immediately after the benediction so that the blessings not be in vain.[13] Solomon Luria recited three verses each from the Torah, Prophets, and Holy Writings.[14]

*Elohai Neshama* ("My God, the soul which Thou hast given me")[15] is said. This prayer is from the Talmud. In some orders of service, it is said after the blessing "Who hast formed man in wisdom," and the study blessings are deferred until the reading of the sacrificial portions from the Torah and talmudic works. In discussing *Elohai Neshama*, the Talmud says:

> When he awakens, he says: "My God, the soul which Thou hast placed in me is pure. Thou hast fashioned it in me. Thou didst breathe it into me, Thou preservest it within me, and Thou wilt in the future take it from me and restore it to me in time to come. As long as the soul is within me I give thanks unto Thee, O Lord, my God, and God of my fathers, Sovereign of all worlds, Lord of all souls. Praised are Thou, O Lord, Who restorest souls to the dead."[16]

Up to this point, the prayers have been said at home. If one attends the Morning Service at the synagogue, he defers all the remaining prayers until that time. Upon entering the synagogue, one recites *Ma Tovu* ("How goodly are your tents," Num. 24:5). The Rabbis interpreted the word *tents* to mean synagogues.[17] The final verse of the selection is: "As for me, my prayer is offered at an acceptable time" (Ps. 69:14). The Talmud states that the appropriate time for prayer is when the community worships.[18]

After *Ma Tovu*, the hymns *Adon Olam* and *Yigdal* are recited silently. *Adon Olam* expresses the acceptance by the worshiper of the Kingship of God. It is one of the best-known hymns in the liturgy. The wording is appropriate for the early part of the Morning Service because it establishes a reverential mood and also alludes to the time of awakening: "Into His Hand I commit my spirit when I sleep and when I awake." That wording establishes *Adon Olam* as a night hymn, too, and it also concludes the bedtime prayer.[19] The word *olam* has two meanings: time and space. *Olam* can mean eternity or universe. Thus, *Adon Olam* can mean "Eternal Lord" or "Lord of the Universe." The hymn not only opens the service, but also is repeated at the conclusion of the service. It is usually sung at the close of the service on Sabbath and holiday mornings. The concept is a common one in Jewish tradition. Opening and closing the service with *Adon Olam* demonstrates the continuity of God's concern for man and continuity of Jewish tradition, just as on Simchat Torah, the reading of the Torah is completed with the final verses of Deuteronomy and is followed immediately by the chanting of the first chapter of Genesis.

The hymn *Yigdal* ("May He be magnified") is recited after *Adon Olam* in most rites. It is based on the Thirteen Articles of Faith of Maimonides. The Ashkenazic version has thirteen lines, one for each article. The Sefardim add a fourteenth line, which reads: "These are the thirteen bases of the rule of Moses, the tenets of his faith." It is usually sung at the close of evening services on Sabbaths and holidays.

Up to this point the prayers have been recited silently. The balance of the preliminary prayers are now recited with the congregation. The public prayer starts with the recitation of several benedictions aloud with the congregation responding *Amen*. They are substantially taken from the Talmud.[20] In summary they praise God for giving man understanding, for opening the eyes of the blind, for loosening the bound, for clothing the naked, for raising up the bowed, for spreading the earth on the waters, for making firm the steps of man, for supplying man's wants, for girding Israel with might, for crowning Israel with glory, and for removing the bands of sleep from the eyes. The series ends with a beautiful prayer:

> May it be Thy will, O Lord, my God, to familiarize me with Thy law and make me cleave to Thy commandments, and do not bring me into sin, or into iniquity or into temptation, or into contempt, and let not the evil inclination have control of me, and remove me from a bad man and a bad companion, and make me cleave to the good inclination and to a good companion in Thy world, and let me obtain this day and every day, grace, favor, and mercy in Thine eyes, and in the eyes of all that see me, and show lovingkindness unto me. Praised art Thou, O Lord, Who bestowest lovingkindness upon Thy people Israel.

From the contents and the context of the benedictions, it appears that the blessings were originally recited at home as various events occurred: awakening, washing, and dressing. Some benedictions have been added to those mentioned in the Talmud. One is "Who gives strength to the weary."

Three others have been a source of controversy and apologia through the ages. They are: "Praised art Thou ... Who has not made me a heathen; ... Who has not made me a slave; Who has not made me a woman." Women say: "Praised art Thou ... Who has made me according to His will." These benedictions are taken from the Talmud.[21] The Jerusalem Talmud mentions another version. Rabbi Judah said that there are

> three things a man must say each day: Praised is he Who has not made me a gentile; praised is He Who has not made me a boor; praised is He Who has not made me a woman. The first because gentiles have no standing before Him; the second because a brutish man does not fear sin; the third because women are not commanded to perform the *mitzvot.*[22]

Rabbi David de Sola Pool in the Sefardic prayerbook translated the benediction "Who has not made me a woman" according to the understanding of the Jerusalem Talmud, i.e., "Who has set upon me the obligations of a man."[23]

Those three benedictions—at least the two relating to non-Jews and women—have been subjected to intense criticism.[24] The plain meaning is that women and non-Jews are inferior. The traditional response is that the benedictions are based on religious obligation. Thus, a Jewish male is bound to perform more commandments than a non-Jew, who according to Jewish law is mandated to observe only the Seven Commandments of the Sons of Noah; a woman (and a non-Jewish slave in ancient times) is obligated to observe only negative commandments of the Torah and those positive commandments that are not time-oriented. A male, therefore, has greater opportunities to serve his Creator, according to Jewish tradition, and praises God for that reason. One reason advanced for the rule relating to women is that a woman is occupied with care of the home and family, which Jewish tradition values highly. She is performing in that view a great *mitzva* and is relieved of time-fixed commandments, pursuant to the rule that "one who is engaged in the performance of a *mitzva* is exempt from other religious duties."[25]

The preliminary service then continues with a group of private prayers and selections from the Torah and Oral Law.

1. The prayer "May it be Thy will . . . to deliver me this day" is from a prayer of Rabbi Judah the Prince.[26]

2. In some prayerbooks the story of the binding of Isaac (Gen. 22:1-19) follows. It tells of Abraham's devotion to God. A closing selection from the Rosh ha-Shana *Musaf* service, "Master of the World," petitions God to judge Israel by the merit of Abraham, who set aside his personal desires to serve Him. The doctrine of *zechut avot* ("merits of the forefathers") is frequently emphasized by Jews in prayer. God is beseeched to answer the supplications of Israel because of the good qualities of the forefathers.

3. The prayers "At all times let a man revere God in private" through "When I bring back your captivity before your eyes, saith the Lord"[27] were instituted when public worship was forbidden to Jews in the 5th century. This summary was a substitute for the Morning Service and thus contains the declaration of *Shema Yisra'el.* The portion, "What are we? What is our life?" was taken from the Yom Kippur *Ne'ila* service.[28] Another possible

reason for the retention of the first sentence of the *Shema* (some prayerbooks carry the entire first paragraph of the *Shema*) early in the service is to permit recitation of the *Shema* in its proper time. The Talmud relates[29] that Rabbi Judah recited the first verse of the *Shema* so that the statutory time would not pass without his having recited at least the first sentence.

4. The next passages relate to the sacrificial system. They contain selections from the Torah relating to the daily offering and the incense offering (Num. 28:1-8 and Exod. 30:34-36 and 30:7-8) and quotations from the Mishna and Gemara relating to the incense offering and the place and sequence of the sacrifices.[30] It is said that the fifth chapter of the Mishna in Tractate Zevachim is recited because it not only deals with the sacrifices, but also is one of the few chapters in the Mishna in which there is no split of opinion among the Rabbis.[31] Recitation of the sacrificial passages serves two purposes. It serves as a study session so that the Torah blessings recited earlier are not in vain. For that reason some prayerbooks place the Torah blessings immediately before those selections. The second reason is that, according to Jewish tradition, recitation of the sacrificial passages constitutes a symbolic offering of the prescribed sacrifices. The Talmud relates that when Abraham foresaw that the Temple would be destroyed, he worried lest Israel in the future lose that means of atonement. God consoled him by saying: "Whenever they study the portions concerning the sacrifices, I shall account it as though they had offered sacrifices before Me, and I will forgive them their sins."[32]

5. The preliminary section closes with the reading of the thirteen rules of Rabbi Ishmael, from the introduction to the *Sifra*, a tannaitic midrash on Leviticus. The rules deal with methods of interpreting the Torah. The rules of Rabbi Ishmael were added to the prayer service in the time of Sa'adia (882-942) to counteract the contentions of the Karaites, who denied the authority of the Oral Law.[33]

## Preliminary Blessings

The entire section ends with a quotation from the Mishna,[34] "May it be Thy Will... that the Temple be rebuilt speedily in our day," and the verse from Malachi 3:4, "And may the offerings of Judah and Jerusalem be pleasant to the Lord as in the days of old and as in former years." The Rabbinic *Kaddish* is then recited.

In some congregations, prior to *Pesukei de-Zimra*, Psalm 30 is said. It carries a superscription, "A Psalm, a Song at the Dedication of the House, a Psalm of David." It is a song of gratitude for recovery from danger or illness. It is a song of victory. As such, it is out of place as a routine prayer. One view is that the psalm was introduced at this point for recitation on Chanuka, when it would be appropriate. Thereafter, either intentionally or because the printer omitted directions, the psalm was recited daily. Joseph Hertz mentions that recitation is optional.[35] A further reason that the recitation was retained was to afford mourners an early opportunity in the service to recite the Mourners' *Kaddish*.

# 7.

# PESUKEI DE-ZIMRA— VERSES OF SONG

THIS PORTION OF THE MORNING SERVICE consists of a series of psalms and other scriptural selections. Its purpose is to prepare the worshiper's mood for recitation of the *Shema* and the *Amida,* the basic morning prayers. The name *Pesukei de-Zimra* ("Verses of Song") is used by Ashkenazim, while Sefardim refer to the selections as *Zemirot* ("Songs").

Recitation of this portion is based on the following traditions:

1. The early pious ones used to pause and meditate for an hour before the formal prayers so as to put themselves in a proper reverential mood.[1] It may be that during that hour, they recited psalms. For example, Rabbi Jose stated: "May my portion be with those who complete the *Hallel* each day."[2] Rashi explained that the statement referred to Psalms 149 and 150, which are now part of the *Pesukei de-Zimra.*[3] Maimonides said that the sages praised those who recited portions of the book of Psalms each day from *Ashrei* (Ps. 145) through the end of the book (Ps. 150).[4]

2. It has always been the Jewish prayer format to praise God first and then ask for one's needs. "A man should first order [i.e., recite] the praises of the Holy One and thereafter pray."[5]
3. One was not to recite the *Amida* while in a sorrowful mood. Recitation of the psalms was instituted to establish a proper frame of mind for prayer, a feeling of *simcha shel mitzva,* joy associated with the performance of a *mitzva.* Rashi explained that reading *Ashrei* before the *Mincha Amida* or the words of redemption *(ga'al Yisra'el)* at the other services put the worshiper in the proper frame of mind.[6] It was an early practice to recite Psalm 145 *(Ashrei)* three times a day.[7] Added to Rabbi Jose's practice previously mentioned, recitation of Psalms 145 through 150 each morning became a regular practice.[8]

As early as Sa'adia (882-942), recitation of *Pesukei de-Zimra* was voluntary. In the time of Rabbi Meir of Rothenberg (13th century), *Pesukei de-Zimra* was formally incorporated into the Morning Service.

In the Ashkenazic prayer service, *Pesukei de-Zimra* is preceded by *Baruch she-Amar* and concludes with *Yishtabach.* In the Sefardic service, a collection of verses known as *Hodu* precedes *Baruch she-Amar.* The latter prayer was apparently composed in the 9th century and is found in Amram Gaon's prayerbook. The first part of the prayer is a hymn praising God. The second part contains a benediction. *Baruch she-Amar* and *Yistabach* are considered as one benediction and therefore, one is forbidden to interrupt his recitation of *Pesukei de-Zimra* except for urgent reasons.[9]

Some expressions in *Baruch she-Amar* are of talmudic and midrashic origin. For example, the words "He Who spoke and the world came into being" is from Sanhedrin 19a, while the phrase "Blessed is He Who has mercy on the creatures of the land" is found in the Mishna (Ta'anit 2:4). In the Ashkenazic service, the prayer has eighty-seven words, the number spelling *PaZ,* pure gold, in Hebrew.[10] The Sefardic rite has different versions of varying length. The prayer was traditionally chanted in a melodious tune and was at times recited responsively, the words *Baruch Hu* ("Blessed is He") serving as the response to various other phrases.[11] In the weekday service of the Ashkenazim, *Pesukei de-Zimra* consists of:

1. *Baruch she-Amar*
2. *Hodu*
3. Psalm 100—Psalm of Thanksgiving
4. *Yehi Kevod*
5. *Ashrei* (Psalm 145)
6. The Hallelujah psalms (146-150)
7. *Baruch Adonai le-Olam* ("Blessed is the Lord")
8. *Va-Yevarech David* ("And David blessed")
9. *Va-Yosha* ("And He saved")
10. *Az Yashir*—The Song of Moses
11. *Yishtabach*

The Half *Kaddish* is then recited to signify the close of a section of the service.

Numbers 1, 3, 7, 8, 9, 10, and 11 are recited while standing. As one recites *Baruch she-Amar*, he holds the two front fringes of the *talit*, and at the close, he kisses and releases them. Some say that *Ashrei* should be recited while sitting because the opening words are "Happy are they who dwell [literally, 'sit'] in Thy house."

*Hodu* consists of verses selected from each of the books of Psalms and from 1 Chronicles 16:8-36, the prayer of David before the Ark. The first fifteen verses of Psalm 105 were incorporated into 1 Chronicles 16:8-22. Psalm 100 is variously known as "A Psalm of Thanksgiving" or "A Psalm for the Thanksgiving Offering," because it was associated with the sacrifices. In a few concise verses, it issues a call to God's service to all peoples, that service to be in a spirit of joy and thanksgiving. It is appropriate to mention the rabbinical statement that, whereas in the future all prayers and sacrifices will cease, those of thanksgiving will continue.[12]

Psalm 100, because of its sacrificial associations, is not recited on the Sabbath, holidays, Passover eve, the intermediate days of Passover, and Yom Kippur eve. The major omission is based on the facts that the Thanksgiving offering was a private not a community sacrifice and, therefore, was not to be brought on Sabbaths and holidays. It is not recited on Passover or Passover eve because the offering was accompanied by loaves of unleavened bread. It is not recited on Yom Kippur eve because the offering could be eaten through the following day, which would conflict with the fast.[13]

Another reason for omitting the Psalm in the Sabbath and holiday liturgy is that those days are considered days of thanksgiving. Psalm 92, recited on the Sabbath and holidays, opens with the words "A psalm, a song, for the Sabbath day. It is a good thing to give thanks unto the Lord." Thus, it was considered a thanksgiving hymn displacing Psalm 100 for those days.[14]

Some Sefardic prayerbooks retain Psalm 100 for Sabbaths and holidays, and some Ashkenazic authorities recited it as well, but omitted the title verse. They believed that the psalm was properly recited even on Sabbaths and holidays because it calls on Israel to acknowledge the goodness of God. For that reason, it fittingly follows *Hodu,* whose final verse contains the words, "I will sing unto the Lord because He has done good things for me" (Ps. 13:6). The Sefardim recite it prior to *Baruch she-Amar* so as to make it part of the recitation of the sacrificial portions. Authorship of the psalm has been attributed to Moses.[15]

*Yehi Kevod* is a collection of verses from the Psalms. Each book, except the second, is represented.

*Ashrei* is Psalm 145 with two verses added before (Ps. 84:5 and 144:5), which account for the name of the prayer, and one verse added at the end, namely, "But we will bless the Lord from this time forth and forever. Hallelujah" (Ps. 115:18). The final verse hints at the World-to-Come and is support for the talmudic maxim that "whoever recites the psalm Praise of David thrice daily is assured of inheriting the World-to-Come."[16] The Talmud interprets *yoshevei* in verse 84:5 literally as "sitting"—thus, "Happy are they who sit in Thy house" referred to the pious men of old who tarried in the synagogue.[17]

Psalm 145 was considered so important because it speaks of God's providence and concern for His creatures. Verse 16 states: "Thou openest Thy hand and satisfiest every living thing with favor." It may be that the two preliminary verses were added because the word *ashrei* occurs three times, thus serving as a reminder that the psalm was to be said three times a day. The addition of the final verse ending with *Hallelujah* may have been to serve as a lead-in to the Hallelujah series of Psalms 146-150, thereby tying in the essential verses of praise, or *Hallel*, earlier alluded to by Rabbi Jose, who asked that his portion be among those who completed the *Hallel* each day. Psalms 146-150 conclude the complete book of Psalms.

*Baruch Adonai le-Olam* is a brief paragraph composed of four verses selected from Psalms. The first verse is the final verse of Book Three (Ps. 89:53). The third and fourth verses, i.e., Psalm 72:18-19, in effect end Book Two. (It is believed that verse 20, which actually completes the psalm, is a postscript.)[18] Thus, the collection of verses serves as a conclusion to the *Hallel* spoken of by Rabbi Jose.

*Va-Yevarech David* consists of a benediction by David from 1 Chronicles 29:10-13. This selection and the succeeding ones were introduced into the service during the geonic period to be representative of the types of praises offered to God. They served as a prelude to *Yishtabach*, the closing paragraph of *Pesukei de-Zimra*. The prayer is recited standing because David did so (1 Chron. 28:2). The kabbalist commentators, based on a custom of Rabbi Isaac Luria, recommend that the worshiper give charity while reciting this prayer and saying the words, ". . . in Thy hand is the power and the strength."[19] Others say that when one comes to the words, "and Thou rulest over all," he should give charity as did Rabbi Luria. The custom was for the *gabbai* to circulate with the charity box or place it in front of the worshipers.[20]

Following *Va-Yevarech David* are five verses from Nehemiah 9:6-11, *Ata Hu* ("Thou art the One"). Those five verses lead into the prayers that follow relating to the wonders of God in leading the Israelites through the Red Sea and in redeeming them. Verse 8 is divided by a pause after the words, "and found his heart faithful before Thee" and prior to the words, "and made a covenant with him." Although it is not considered proper to recite parts of verses as prayers ("We must not divide any verse that was not divided by Moses," Ta'anit 27b), this rule applies only to verses from the Torah and the Prophets, but not to verses from the Holy Writings, of which the book of Nehemiah is a part. The practice of dividing verse 8 began when there was a circumcision to be performed at the synagogue. The portions mentioning the Covenant were emphasized and chanted in a special manner. The custom of dividing the verse continued even when there was no circumcision.[21] The portion starting *Ata Hu* is recited by Ashkenazim while standing because Nehemiah so states (Neh. 9:3-5). Sefardim are seated through *Yishtabach*.

Thereafter follow the verses *Va-Yosha* (Exod. 11:30-31) and the Song of Moses (Exod. 15:1-18), relating to the redemption. Verse 18 is repeated, as is customary to signify the close of the Song. Added thereto are three verses—Psalms 22:29, Obadiah 1:21, and Zechariah 14:9: "For the kingdom is the Lord's," "And saviors shall come up on Mount Zion . . . , and the Kingdom shall be the Lord's," and "And the Lord shall be King over all the earth." Some prayerbooks add the verse "Hear, O Israel," an Aramaic translation of the last verse of the Song of Moses, and another verse.

A reason given for repeating verse 18 of the Song of Moses and adding the three verses from Psalms, Obadiah, and Zechariah was to bring the number of times God's Name is mentioned to eighteen. Because the Name has four letters, the sum of the letters would be seventy-two, which is the number of letters or syllables in a kabbalistic formulation of God's Name. Moses was said to have learned the secret Name at the Burning

Bush and recited it to split the Red Sea.[22] For that reason the verses of "Hear, O Israel" should not be added because they would change the count.

The three verses that are added from Psalms, Obadiah, and Zechariah introduce the theme of the universality of God's Kingship, which emphasizes that God not only redeemed the Jews and ruled over them, but that He is the Ruler of all mankind.

*Yishtabach* concludes *Pesukei de-Zimra*. It is referred to in the Talmud as the "Benediction of Song."[23] A total of thirteen kinds of praises are mentioned to correspond with the Thirteen Attributes of God. Kabbalistic meaning has been attached to the prayer, and the *Zohar* states that the thirteen praises are to be recited in one breath.[24]

The prayer is recited standing among Ashkenazim.[25] It is a benediction that does not contain mention of God's Kingship, i.e., the words "King of the Universe." To qualify as a proper benediction, it is joined to *Baruch she-Amar*, and as previously mentioned, the entire series of prayers are considered one blessing. As is usual, the Half *Kaddish* is recited after *Yishtabach* to denote that a section of the prayer service has been completed.[26]

# 8.

# KERI'AT SHEMA— THE SHEMA AND ITS BENEDICTIONS

## *Barechu*

*Barechu* is the call to worship. In ancient times the Morning Service proper, consisting of the *Shema* and *Amida*, started at this point.[1]

Like the *Kaddish, Barechu* is considered a matter of sanctification and may be recited only when a *minyan* is present.[2] The reader says: "Praised *(Barechu)* be the Lord, Who is [to be] praised," and the members of the congregation rise, bow their heads and respond: "Praised is the Lord, Who is praised, for ever and ever."

The basic concept is from Nehemiah 9:5:

> Then the Levites ... said: "Stand up and bless *(barechu)* the Lord, your God from everlasting to everlasting, and let them say, 'Blessed be Thy glorious Name, that is exalted above all blessing and praise.'"

That passage also explains why the recitation is said standing.

In the Mishna,[3] it is mentioned that Rabbi Akiba suggested that the formula be "Praise the Lord," while Rabbi Ishmael, whose view was accepted, stated that it should be "Praise the Lord, Who is praised."[4] The prayer leader is required to repeat the response of the congregation. The Talmud states[5] that a man should never exclude himself from the congregation. It was felt that it would be preferable for the leader to say "Let us praise" rather than "Praise," as is done at the recitation of the Grace after Meals. It was finally decided that it would be satisfactory for the leader to say *Barechu*, "Praise," if he then repeated the congregational response so as to include himself within the group's declaration.

It is customary in some places to recite silently the short selection "May He be blessed and praised...," while the reader says the *Barechu*.[6]

## The Reading of the Shema

### Introduction

After *Barechu*, the worshiper recites the two benedictions preceding the *Shema*.[7] The first is *Yotzer Or*, "Who creates light," and the second is *Ahava Rabba*, "With abounding love."

In addition to the two preceding blessings, the *Shema* is followed by one benediction in the Morning Service—*Emet ve-Yatziv*, "True and firm," which includes mention of the liberation from Egypt. The underlying themes of the three benedictions are: (1) Creation, (2) Revelation, and (3) Redemption. The concept has a partial source in Psalm 19, where first the luminaries were mentioned and then Torah.[8]

Halevi states that when a worshiper recites the first blessing, "Who creates the lights," he recognizes the order in the celestial world, the greatness of the heavenly bodies and their usefulness, and he also understands that the heavenly bodies are no different from

God's other creations. When the worshiper recites the second benediction, "With [everlasting] love" ("With abounding love" in the Ashkenazic rite), he realizes the connection of the Divine power with the community which is to receive that love and understands that the Torah is the outcome of God's desire to reveal His dominion on earth as in heaven.[9] Thereafter the worshiper takes upon himself the yoke of Divine law and recites the *Shema*.

The blessing following the *Shema*, "True and firm," then serves as a confirmation of the acknowledgment of the Torah, and the worshiper affirms his belief in the sovereignty and eternity of God as well as the providential care bestowed upon Israel's forefathers. The proof is the redemption from Egypt. At that point, says Halevi, the worshiper is prepared to recite the *Amida*.[10]

## *First Benediction*

The first blessing starts, "Who creates light and darkness, makes peace and creates everything." It is worded this way because one must mention the attributes of night during the day and those of day at night.[11] The specific wording is from a verse in Isaiah 45:7, with a variation. The prophet states in the name of God that "I form light and create darkness, make peace and create evil." The prayer changes the ending to "all things." This alteration is done for purposes of euphemism.[12] It is Jewish tradition to avoid expressions involving misfortune.

There is more to the verse from Isaiah and the first benediction than appears on the surface. Both the prophet and the author of the benediction were stressing a monotheistic concept and were denying a system of multiple divinities with different functions and powers.

On the surface, the first benediction praises God for the daily renewal of the order of creation and its luminaries.[13] Halevi points out that the first blessing was a polemic against those who worshiped heavenly luminaries. Thus, when the Jews praised God as Creator of the sun, moon, and stars, they were placing those bodies in perspective as creations of God, just like insects.[14] Furthermore, affirmation by implication of God's Unity serves as a fitting preliminary to the *Shema.*

The first blessing originally was short and consisted of Israel's praises of God for renewal of creation. Sometime later an allusion was made to the praises uttered by the angels, who, according to Jewish folklore, praise God each day, as do earthly creatures. A narrative of heavenly worship was included in the first benediction. The angels recite the trisagion, "Holy, Holy, Holy." It is known as the *Kedusha de-Yotzer,* the sanctification prayer of the benediction of lights.[15] Thereafter, the prayer returns to the praises recited by earthlings and asks God to cause a new light to shine on Zion. It concludes with a benediction praising God as Creator of lights.

The selection about the angels and the reference to a new light interrupt the literary continuity of the first benediction. A question was raised whether one praying without a *minyan* should recite the *Kedusha de-Yotzer.* The regular *Kedusha* may not be recited without a *minyan* because God may be truly sanctified only in the presence of a congregation. The Talmud states[16] that the verse, "And I shall be sanctified amongst the children of Israel" (Lev. 22:32), means that all matters relating to the sanctification of God must take place in the presence of not less than ten men. For that reason, some authorities (Maimonides, for example) ruled that the *Kedusha* section of the first benediction should be omitted when one prays alone.[17] (It was later stated by Maimonides' son that his father had retracted that statement and followed the prevailing view that a *minyan* was not necessary, since one was merely restating a narrative of the angels and was not himself sanctifying God. The same rule was applied to the *Kedusha* in *U-Va le-Tziyon.)*

Of interest are two versions of the sentence, "And they all take upon themselves . . . and give leave one to the other to declare the holiness of their Creator . . . with pure speech and holy melody. . . ." One reading is, *u-vine'ima kedosha*—"and in holy melody." The other is *u-vine'ima, Kedusha*—"and in pleasant melody, *Kedusha* they respond." The Ba'er Heitev[18] follows the former, as do the Hertz, Silverman, Pool, and Birnbaum prayerbooks. The second is found in many prayerbooks, including the Sabbath *siddur* of the Rabbinical Council of America.

The Sefardic rite does not use the expression, "O cause a new light to shine on Zion," because it introduces a new thought unconnected with creation. Sa'adia Gaon omitted it. The Rosh (d. 1327) in his responsa favored insertion of the phrase. He noted that it referred to the primordial light stored up by God at creation for the righteous in the World-to-Come.[19]

## Second Benediction

The second blessing of the morning *Shema* is *Ahava Rabba*, "With abounding love," in the Ashkenazic rite. In the evening the second blessing is *Ahavat Olam*, "With everlasting love." In the Sefardic rite, *Ahavat Olam* is recited both mornings and evenings, although the morning version is extended and substantially parallels the content of *Ahava Rabba*. The two versions are the result of a talmudic debate as to the proper prayer. The Ashkenazim, in a spirit of compromise, reserved one version for the morning and other for the evening.[20]

*Ahava Rabba* is an ancient prayer, which the priests recited in Temple times. They did not recite *Yotzer Or* because they prayed before daybreak.[21]

While the first benediction speaks of God as Creator, the second focuses on God and His relationship with Israel, to whom He gave the Torah. The themes of Torah and God's love for Israel through revelation are expressed as well as Israel's gratitude. *Ahava Rabba* in its emphasis on Torah and study is considered a Torah benediction. If one has not recited the benediction on Torah study in the preliminary service, his recitation of *Ahava Rabba* suffices for that purpose.[22] Both the Torah blessing and *Ahava Rabba* contain ideas of revelation and Israel's selection as God's people.

One writer states that the benediction expresses God's love and compassion through teaching Israel the statutes of life. He notes that the blessing anticipates the *Shema* in its aspect of study of Torah and in its acknowledgment of the Kingdom of Heaven.[23]

A question frequently asked is why a special benediction of the formula, "Who has sanctified us in His commandments and commanded us to . . . ," is not recited before reading the *Shema*. One answer is that the two preliminary blessings serve the purpose. Maharam Schick (19th century), in a responsum[24] on this question, stated that a *beracha* was to be recited before performance of a *mitzva* only where it was certain that the *mitzva* will be performed. Since *kavana* is required to fulfill reading of the *Shema*, one can never be certain beforehand that he will properly perform the commandment. He therefore does not recite a benediction on reading of the *Shema*.

## The Shema

The Reading of the *Shema*, or *Keri'at Shema*, consists of three paragraphs: 1. *Shema* (Deut. 6:4-9); 2. *Vehaya im shamoa* (Deut. 11:13-21); 3. *Va-yomer* (Num. 15:37-41).

It is not a prayer in the sense of supplication. It is an affirmation of faith in the One God, Who rules the world and fixes the measure of man's conduct. From that principle all else in Judaism flows. Just as God is One, so is Israel one. The Sabbath afternoon *Amida* contains the phrase, "Thou art One and Thy Name is One and who is like Thy people Israel, one nation on earth."

In the Torah scroll, the word *shema* ("Hear") has a large *ayin*, and the word *echad* ("One") has a large *dalet*— spelling the word *ed* ("witness"). Israel is witness to God's Unity and Oneness. A more plausible reason for the enlarged letters was to avoid error in reading and pronunciation. A change in the last letter of the word *shema* could cause it to be read: *shema* ("perhaps"). Unless the form of the *dalet* were clear, it could be mistaken for a *resh*, and the reading would be *acher* ("another"). (The same problem arises with another verse [Exod. 34:14] which reads, "For you shall not bow down to another God." "Another," *acher*, has a large *resh* so that it will not be read as, *echad*, "one."[25])

The first sentence of the *Shema* is translated as "Hear, O Israel: The Lord our God, the Lord is One," and as "Hear, O Israel, the Lord is our God, the Lord is One." Rashi states that the verse means that the Eternal, Who is our God and not the God of the other nations, will eventually be acknowledged as the One and only God, as it is said, "in that day shall the Eternal be One and His Name One" (Zech. 14:19, incorporated in the *Aleinu*).[26] Rashi further points out that this is the special meaning of the verse because the Unity of God was already made clear in the Ten Commandments.[27]

Ramban (Nachmanides, 1194-1270) comments on the use of the words *our God*. Inasmuch as Moses was speaking, he might have said to Israel, *your God*, but he did not want to exclude himself from the declaration of God's Unity. Later he returned to the second person, "You shall love, etc."

It is interesting to consider why this most important verse commences with *Shema* ("Hear"), rather than *Re'eh* ("See"), as in some other verses. It may be that the sense of hearing provides a more penetrating means of communication and perception than the sense of sight. Apparently something heard awakens greater emotion and feeling than does something seen.[28]

Reik has written that

> the auditory sphere may claim an exceptional position in the development of the superego of the individual.... Purely optical impressions without words by themselves would be insufficient for the establishment of ethical judgments. For the preliminary stages of superego formation, language audibly perceived is indispensable.[29]

Thus the all-important message of God's Unity had to be perceived by hearing, not sight.

Many customs and traditions invest the recitation of the verse, "Hear, O Israel." It is recited aloud with the eyes closed and a hand covering them as an aid to concentration. That practice was a custom of R. Judah the Prince, of whom the Talmud relates:[30] He passed his hand over his eyes in concentration and accepted the Kingdom of Heaven. It became the prevailing custom.[31]

The Talmud insists that at least the first verse, "Hear, O Israel," must be recited with *kavana*, concentration, and intent to declare the Unity of God.[32] The utterance of the word *echad* ("One") is prolonged, apparently to aid concentration and to allow one to proclaim God's Unity and Majesty.[33] In Berachot, Symmachos says that he who prolongs *echad* prolongs his days and years. Rabbi Jeremiah was once sitting before Rabbi Chiya bar Abba. He saw that he was prolonging the *echad* very much. He said to him: "Once you have proclaimed His Kingship above and below and over the four directions of heaven, no more is required."[34]

The Talmud further states that use of the word *Shema* ("Hear") means that the reading may be in any language, not necessarily in Hebrew. Another view was that the word *Shema* taught that the reading must be loud enough that the worshiper may hear his own words.[35]

Abudraham (14th century) by use of *notarikon* (a type of abbreviation) created a play on the spelling of the word *shema—shin, mem, ayin*—and taught a lesson about prayer. He said: *shin, mem, ayin* mean *Se'u Marom Eineichem*—"Lift your eyes on high" (Isa. 40:26). To whom? *Shaddai Melech Elyon*—"The Almighty, King above (on high)." When? *Shacharit, Mincha, Arvit*— "Morning, afternoon, and night."

The first verse may be recited standing still or sitting or in any respectful position.³⁶ In Orthodox synagogues, it is said sitting down. In Conservative and Reform synagogues, the congregation rises to emphasize the importance of the first verse. The Jerusalem Talmud states that one should accept the yoke of the Heavenly Kingdom while standing, but one should not rise from a sitting position.³⁷ The *Shulchan Aruch* says that one should not rise from a sitting position to recite the first verse. Mishna Berura explains that it gives the impression of arrogance, that one is trying to show that he is very devout.³⁸

## *El Melech Ne'eman*

When one does not recite the *Shema* at the same time the congregation does, he adds a preliminary *El Melech Ne'eman*, "God Faithful King." There are numerous reasons given for this practice:

1. When one prays alone, he misses the opportunity to say *Amen* after the *Ahava Rabba* prayer.³⁹ The initial letters of *El Melech Ne'eman* spell *Amen*.⁴⁰

2. The second reason is a kabbalistic one. Traditionally the reading of the *Shema* must contain 248 words. The *Shema* itself contains 245 words. When one recites it with the congregation, the reader repeats the last three words: *Adonai Eloheichem Emet*, "The Lord your God is True." One who prays alone must compensate for those last three words by adding the three words at the start. The significance of the number 248 is that the Rabbis concluded that there are 248 organs of the body. Midrash Tanchuma, Kedoshim⁴¹, says: "If you observe the 248 words of the *Shema* and read them properly, I will preserve the 248 organs of the body."

3. Louis Ginzberg contends that God Faithful King is a remnant of a complete benediction over reading the *Shema,* formerly recited by individuals at private prayer.[42]

4. Israel Abrahams gives the following explanation. The first paragraph of the *Shema* represents the acceptance of the yoke of the Kingdom of Heaven,[43] but it does not expressly say so. Thus the Rabbis instituted the recitation of *Baruch Shem Kevod* ("Praised be the Name of His glorious majesty for ever and ever") immediately after the first verse. *Baruch Shem Kevod,* he says, was a public, not a private, response, used in the Holy Temple.[44] How then could a private individual praying alone accept the Kingdom of God in reciting the *Shema?* The answer was by saying "God Faithful King."[45]

After recitation of the first verse, one recites the verse, *Baruch Shem Kevod,* mentioned above, in a whisper, except on Yom Kippur. There are various traditions for this practice. As already mentioned, the verse was probably included in the *Shema* to make clear the concept of God's Majesty and Kingship. The verse is based on Nehemiah 9:5.

1. One legend has it that Moses heard the angels recite *Baruch Shem . . . ,* and believing it to be a fitting verse, ordained that it be recited after the first verse of the *Shema,* but in a whisper so as not to cause enmity with the heavenly creatures. On Yom Kippur, however, Israelites are on a par with the angels and may recite the verse aloud.[46]

2. Another tradition, mentioned by the Talmud and Maimonides is that Jacob, near death, inquired of his children about their faith. They replied: "Hear, O Israel [a name for Jacob], the Lord our God . . . ," to which Jacob replied: *"Baruch Shem Kevod . . . ."* The response was then incorporated into the *Keri'at Shema,* but was recited in a whisper because it was not part of the Torah text.[47] But this does not explain why *Baruch Shem* is recited aloud on Yom Kippur. One reason may be that *Baruch Shem,* used in Temple times as a response to a

benediction, as *Amen* now is, was recited particularly on Yom Kippur,[48] and it is therefore said aloud on that day. The Mishna recounts that after the High Priest had laid his hands on the scapegoat and confessed the sins of the House of Israel, reciting the Name of God, the priests and the people in the Temple court used to kneel, bow down, and fall down on their faces and say: "Praised be the Name of the glory of His majesty for ever and ever."[49]

3. Another reason may be that, because *Baruch Shem* is a declaration of God's Kingship, it was considered an act of treason in some foreign lands to express one's belief in God's sovereignty over that of a mortal monarch. To avoid harassment, Jews decided to whisper the verse. This is not too valid a reason, inasmuch as the *Shema* was recited aloud, and the Jews were punished for reciting it.[50]

## *Contents of the Shema*

The paragraphs of the *Shema* are not in sequence as found in the Torah. The Talmud[51] explains the order used in the prayerbook. In the first paragraph, the worshiper accepts the yoke of the Kingdom of Heaven, i.e., he accepts God; in the second paragraph, he accepts the yoke of the commandments, i.e., once God's authority is accepted, then His *mitzvot* follow. The third paragraph as well emphasizes the importance of the commandments.[52]

*Ve-haya,* the second paragraph, precedes *Va-yomer* because *Ve-haya,* calling for Torah study, applies day and night, while *Va-yomer* deals with *tzitzit,* which is obligatory only during the day. (The inclusion of *Va-yomer* in the evening *Keri'at Shema* will be discussed later.)

The three paragraphs of the *Shema* call for an affirmation of the essentials of Judaism.

1. The first paragraph proclaims the Unity and Kingship of God. It stresses love of God and love of Torah; that Torah shall be in the Jew's heart night and day, in all his activities, and that it shall be taught to the chil-

dren. Then the *mitzvot* of *tefilin* and *mezuza* are mandated.

2. The primary theme of the second paragraph is reward and punishment. It repeats some of the statements of the first paragraph and adds the thought that one of the rewards will be length of days.

The first paragraph is phrased in the singular; the second, in the plural. Ramban comments that the individual lives by his own merits, while matters of rain and produce are determined according to the deeds of the majority of the community. In the Jerusalem Talmud it is said:[53] "Wherein do the first and second sections differ from one another.... The first is addressed to the individual; the second to the community. The first calls for study; the second for action."[54]

3. The important themes of the third paragraph are seldom recognized. On the surface, the selection appears to concern itself with the fringes, *tzitzit*, as a reminder of all God's commandments and of the Exodus. A closer analysis discloses mention of five crucial subjects: *tzitzit*, Exodus, acceptance of the yoke of *mitzvot*, warning against heresy and idolatry, and warning against immorality.[55]

The Babylonian Talmud points out[56] that although the priests at a Temple service recited the Ten Commandments along with the *Shema* and other prayers, the reading of the Ten Commandments was prohibited outside the Temple because of the heretics, who insinuated that the Ten Commandments alone were the only valid part of the Torah. Thereafter, reading of the Decalogue was never a part of the statutory service, but the Ten Commandments were alluded to in the three paragraphs of the *Shema*.

The Jerusalem Talmud asks:[57] "Why are these paragraphs recited every day? Said Rabbi Levi: 'Because the Ten Commandments are included therein.'" It then traces the ten in the following manner:

KERI'AT SHEMA

| TEN COMMANDMENTS | SHEMA |
|---|---|
| 1. I am the Lord, Thy God. | 1. Hear, O Israel, the Lord is our God. |
| 2. You shall have no other gods. | 2. The Lord is One. |
| 3. You shall not take the name of the Lord in vain. | 3. You shall love the Lord thy God. |
| 4. Remember (*zachor*) the Sabbath. | 4. So that you shall remember (that means the Sabbath, which is comparable to all the commandments). |
| 5. Honor your mother and father so that your days will be multiplied. | 5. So that your days will be multiplied and the days of your children. |
| 6. Do not murder. | 6. And you shall be lost (one who murders is killed). |
| 7. Do not commit adultery | 7. You shall not turn aside after your heart and your eyes. (Rabbi Levi said the heart and the eyes are two inciters of sin). |
| 8. Do not steal. | 8. You shall gather your corn (and not the corn of another). |
| 9. You shall not bear false witness; I am the Lord Thy God. | 9. The Lord thy God is true. (What is truth, if you bear false witness? It is as though you bore witness that I did not create heaven and earth.) |

| | |
|---|---|
| 10. You shall not covet the house of your brother, his wife . . . | 10. And you shall write them on the doorposts of your house (and not on that of your brother). |

In public worship, after the congregation has recited the *Shema*, the reader concludes aloud with the three words: *Adonai Eloheichem Emet,* "The Lord Thy God is True." The first two words of the phrase are the last two words of the *Shema* with the word *emet* added. The three-word expression is found in Jeremiah 10:10, but its usage here is based on a passage in the *Zohar Chadash*.[58] The three-word phrase serves as a lead-in to the benediction after the morning *Shema—Emet ve-Yatziv,* "True and firm."

## Benedictions After Shema

The Talmud states[59] that one must recite *Emet ve-Yatziv* in the morning and *Emet ve-Emuna* at night. *Emet ve-Yatziv* is the redemption prayer and refers back to the *Shema* and affirms that all of it is true and correct. It is an old selection recited by the priests in the Temple.[60] Rashi explains[61] that *Emet ve-Yatziv* speaks of past lovingkindness of God shown to our forefathers in that He took them from Egypt, divided the sea for them, and caused them to cross over. The Jerusalem Talmud says[62] that the Exodus must be mentioned in *Emet ve-Yatziv*, as well as the division of the Red Sea, and the plague of the firstborn.

The benediction ends with the recitation of the redemption from Egypt—a past event. It should be noted that the blessing is in the past tense, while a similar benediction in the *Amida* is in the present tense. It should also be noted that the benediction does not start with *baruch* and does not contain mention of God's Kingship. It, therefore, meets the formal requirements for a *beracha* by referring back to the first benediction before the *Shema—Yotzer Or.*

It was ordained by the Rabbis that immediately upon recitation of the blessing "Who has redeemed Israel," one must commence the *Amida*. The *Ge'ula* (Redemption) must be joined to the *Tefila (Amida)*.[63]

## Joining Ge'ula to Tefila

What is the great significance of joining the *Ge'ula* to the *Tefila* that Rabbi Jochanan said: "Who is a son of the world to come? He who joins the *Ge'ula* to the *Tefila*."
Here are some possible reasons:

1. Rashi explains[64] with reference to a baraita which held that one should not pray when in a sorrowful mood, that mention of the past redemption will gladden the worshiper's heart and put him in the proper frame of mind to recite the *Amida*.

2. Judah Halevi says that *Emet ve-Yatziv* confirms all that was contained in the *Shema*, and the worshiper thus "binds his soul and asserts that he regards all this as obligatory as his forefathers did...." He further states that the worshiper then affirms his faith in God and the Torah, and concludes with mention of the Exodus from Egypt and the redemption benediction. Halevi explains that, thus fortified, the Jew is worthy to stand before God and pray for his needs.[65] Commenting thereon, Isaac Heinemann says that Halevi means to say that only he who has strengthened himself in the fundamental truths of his faith can hope to be heard.[66]

3. Rabbi Joseph B. Soloveitchik in an essay, "Redemption, Prayer, Talmud Torah," explains as follows: Until redeemed, man is in a state of slavery. He is inarticulate and unaware of his needs. He is incapable of expressing his needs. Once redeemed, he is liberated and becomes articulate. He is then ready for prayer.[67] Thus, Halacha links prayer with redemption.

4. Whatever the reason for joining the *Ge'ula* to the *Tefila*, a result is the creation of a system of three prayer services daily, instead of five. The *Shema* must be recited twice daily. In the morning it must be said by the third

hour after sunrise. At night it must be said from the appearance of three stars to the rise of dawn. The *Amida* must be recited three times a day. Its time limit in the morning is until the fourth hour, and at night, any time from late afternoon until the rise of dawn. It is conceivable that there could be five services. By linking the *Shema* to the *Amida,* the services are reduced to three. Heinemann and Petuchowski state:

> The purpose of this ruling [joining the *Ge'ula* to the *Tefila*] presumably was to ensure the recital of both the Shema and the Amidah in the synagogue—a practice that would involve great difficulties if each of them constituted a service; its effect, undoubtedly, was to create a more comprehensive service, consisting at a minimum of these two parts joined together.[68]

5. Rashi gives further explanation.[69] He says that the primary Exodus was in the morning; that King David in the Psalms hinted at the joining of the *Ge'ula* to the *Amida,* because Psalm 19 says, "The Lord is my Rock and my Redeemer," and is followed by the verse in Psalm 20, which says, "He will answer you in the day of trouble." Rashi then cites a passage in the Jerusalem Talmud[70] for the proposition that when reciting the prayers and praises concerning the redemption from Egypt, man brings himself close to God. At that point, it is propitious to pray for his needs. If he delays, he misses his great opportunity.

6. Rabbi Emanuel Rackman states that one becomes aware of God's proximity only after appreciating His intervention in history by parting the waters of the Red Sea. Recitation of the *Ge'ula* prayer before the *Amida* induces in the worshiper an awareness that permits him to approach God intimately and to pray for his needs.[71]

To implement the rabbinic instruction, it has been the practice of the reader to complete the last *beracha, Ga'al Yisra'el,* in an undertone so that the congregation need not answer *Amen* and thus interrupt between the two prayers. Some authorities hold that the reader should say the blessing aloud, but that the individual worshiper should either recite the blessing at the same time or complete it before the reader and start the *Amida* so that in either case he would not be required to say *Amen*.[72]

## *The Ma'ariv Shema*

In the *Ma'ariv* service, the *Shema* has two blessings preceding it and two following it.[73] In some traditions there are now three. The two preceding and the first after follow the same general theme as the morning recitation: Creation and Nature, God's Love for Israel, and Redemption.

The first preceding benediction praises God: "Thou rollest away light before darkness, and the darkness before light."[74] It is explained in the Talmud[75] that the distinctive feature of the day—i.e., light—must be mentioned at night, just as the distinctive feature of night—i.e., darkness—must be mentioned in the first benediction of the morning *Shema*. The obvious reason is to proclaim the Unity of God, and thus dispel any notion of dual creators.

Just as the second benediction before the morning *Shema* focuses on God's love of Israel, so does the second blessing before the evening *Shema*. The evening blessing in the Ashkenazic ritual uses the opening words, *Ahavat Olam* ("With everlasting love"), the alternate phrase mentioned in the Talmud.[76] The Sefardim open the second blessing morning and night with *Ahavat Olam*. The wording of the benediction emphasizes a cardinal rule of Judaism that study of Torah is mandatory day and night.

The phrase "everlasting love" is from Jeremiah 31:2; "We will meditate on Thine statutes" is from Psalms 119:48; "Torah is our life and length of our days" is from Deuteronomy 30:20; the phrase "meditate day and night" is from Joshua 1:8.

Thereafter follow the three paragraphs of the *Shema*. There was a controversy over inclusion of the third paragraph in the Evening Service, inasmuch as it refers to *tzitzit*, which is obligatory only during the day. The decision was to include it because the section speaks of the Exodus from Egypt, which was to be mentioned at night. The principle is reported in the Mishna Berachot, chapter 1, mishna 5 (and made a part of the Passover Haggada): "R. Eleazer b. Azariah said, 'Behold I am like one seventy years old, and I have never been worthy to expound a reason why the Exodus from Egypt should be mentioned at night until Ben Zoma expounded it.'" The rule was deduced from the verse (Deut. 16:3) which mandated remembering the Exodus "all the days of your life." Ben Zoma took the position that the word *all* was superfluous and meant to convey that *days* meant not only daytime but nighttime as well.

The first blessing after the *Shema* is *Emet ve-Emuna*, "True and trustworthy is all this."[77] Like its counterpart in the morning, it speaks of redemption and ends like the morning benediction with "Praised art Thou ... Who hast redeemed Israel."[78]

If one fails to say *Emet ve-Yatziv* in the morning or *Emet ve-Emuna* in the evening, he has not performed his duty, for it is said: "To declare Thy lovingkindness in the morning and Thy faithfulness in the nights" (Ps. 92:3). Rashi explains[79] that while *Emet ve-Yatziv* deals with past kindness of God in redeeming Israel from Egypt, *Emet ve-Emuna* refers to the future and anticipates God's faithfulness and promise to redeem Israel from its oppressors. The benediction is an affirmation of faith that God is our Lord, and that Israel is His people.

The second succeeding blessing is *Hashkivenu*, "Cause us to lie down in peace." It is a prayer for protection at night. It is based on the verse, "God, the Guardian of Israel, neither slumbers, nor sleeps" (Ps. 121:4). There are two versions of the prayer, one of which is reserved for the Sabbath and holidays.

Recitation of *Hashkivenu* and *Baruch Adonai le-Olam* with *Yir'u Eineinu* is not considered an interruption between the *Ge'ula* (Redemption) prayer and the *Amida*, since the two are looked upon as a "long redemption prayer."[80]

The prayer *Baruch Adonai le-Olam* and its placement after *Hashkivenu* are not entirely clear. The view of the Rosh (14th century) was that, because synagogues in olden times were outside the towns and there was nighttime danger to worshipers, the people recited the *Shema* and *Baruch Adonai le-Olam* to complete the prayers before nightfall. They then left for home safely.[81] *Baruch Adonai le-Olam* was considered a substitute for the *Amida* for two reasons: It contains the Name of God eighteen times and has eighteen verses. The *Kaddish* was then recited to conclude the service.[82] Later, the prayer was continued in the service, the final *Kaddish* became a Half *Kaddish,* and the *Amida* was added.

It may be that *Baruch Adonai le-Olam* became part of the Evening Service when the debate existed whether the evening *Amida* was optional.[83] Once it was finally established that the evening *Amida* was obligatory, it was retained. Tosafot to Berachot 4b[84] seems to indicate that *Baruch Adonai le-Olam* was added to prolong the Evening Service so that latecomers would not be left alone, after others left.

Rashi states[85] that the verse "For the Lord will not forsake His people" (1 Sam. 12:22) included in *Baruch Adonai le-Olam* places the worshiper in a proper frame of mind before reciting the *Amida*, as does recitation of *Ashrei* at *Mincha*. The Rashba (R. Solomon ben Adret, 1235-1310) states that the prayer was written in time of religious persecution, when Jews were forbidden to pray. It then served as a substitute for the *Amida* because God's Name is mentioned eighteen times. When the prohibitions were removed, he says, the prayer remained part of the service.[86]

In Israel, the prayer *Baruch Adonai le-Olam* is omitted from the weekday service, and *Hashkivenu* is followed by Half *Kaddish* and the *Amida*. Such was and is the practice of many diaspora scholars, including the Wilna Gaon, and the Sefardic and some Chasidic congregations.

Half *Kaddish* is recited at the end of the final benediction of the evening *Shema* because, as previously mentioned, the *Ma'ariv* service once ended at that point.

# 9.
# THE AMIDA

THE AMIDA, popularly known as the *Shemoneh Esreh,* "The Eighteen Benedictions," is the preeminent prayer. Formulated by the Men of the Great Assembly, it is the focal point of the statutory services. In talmudic times, it was known as The *Tefila,* The Prayer. Later it was called *Amida,* "The Standing Prayer," because ordinarily it should be recited in a standing position.[1] Some refer to it as *Tefila be-Lachash,* "The Silent Devotion," because it must also be said in a whisper.[2]

It was called the *Shemoneh Esreh* because originally the weekday version consisted of eighteen benedictions. (As applied to the holiday or Sabbath prayers, that name is a misnomer because they contain fewer benedictions.) Later a nineteenth blessing was added, or one was divided in two, but the name did not change. Rashi indicates that it was an old prayer.[3] By the time the additional benediction was added, the name *Shemoneh Esreh* was well known and difficult to change. Another reason given is that the nineteenth benediction was added because of unhappy circumstances, the rise of informers and heretics among Jews. The name *Shemoneh Esreh* was retained because of the constant hope that the conditions that brought about the change would cease, that the blessings would once again revert to eighteen, and that the name would once again be *Shemoneh Esreh*.[4]

The structure of the prayer is tripartite:

1. The first three benedictions consist of praises of God, based upon the tradition that before asking for one's needs, one should utter God's praises. R. Simlai said: "A man should always first recount the praises of the Holy One, blessed be He, and then pray for his needs." He cited Moses' prayer in Deuteronomy 3:23.[5]

2. The next thirteen benedictions concern man's needs. This portion is recited only on weekdays, inasmuch as it is forbidden to offer such supplications on the Sabbath or holidays. On those days, the central portion consists of an appropriate reference to the day.

3. The final three benedictions are primarily expressions of thanksgiving to God with a concluding prayer for peace.

The first and third series of blessings are essentially the same at all times. The central portion changes in accordance with the particular holiday. Maimonides explains the three sections as follows: A man should recite the praises of the Holy One; thereafter, he should ask for his needs, and then give praise and thanks to God for the good He has shown him.[6]

The rules dealing with the structure and manner of recitation of the *Amida* rely heavily on the analogies of the worshiper as servant or subject, and God as Master or King. It is clear from talmudic sources that the order of the benedictions and the particular concept of each were set down in talmudic times, but the specific wording was not fixed until later.

## *Preliminary Verse*

An introductory verse preceded the *Amida* since talmudic times. The worshiper paces three steps forward as though entering the presence of an earthly king and recites: "O Lord, open my lips, and my mouth will utter Thy praises" (Ps. 51:17). He then utters the first benediction as he bends the knees and bows his head. The verse is not considered an interruption between the *Ge'ula* and the *Amida*[7] because the worshiper asks for God's help to articulate his prayers. In the Afternoon and *Musaf* Services, this verse is preceded by "When I will proclaim the name of the Lord, ascribe greatness unto our God" (Deut. 32:3).

## First Section

The three benedictions in this section are as follows: 1. *Avot* ("forefathers"), 2. *Gevurot* ("strengths"), and 3. *Kedusha* ("sanctification"). A rationale for reciting the first three benedictions and their sequence is found in the Talmud.[8] It is based on verses in Psalm 29. "Ascribe unto the Lord, O you sons of might" (v. 1) refers to the patriarchs; "Ascribe unto the Lord glory and strength" (v. 1) refers to God's powers; and "Ascribe unto the Lord ... worship the Lord in the beauty of holiness" (v. 2) refers to the sanctification blessing.

In the very first benediction, the worshiper calls upon the God of his forefathers, Abraham, Isaac, and Jacob. The Jew, as he commences the great prayer, summons up *zechut avot,* "the merit of the fathers," and identifies himself with them.[9] In so identifying himself, he expresses to God his unworthiness, and asks that his prayers be answered, not on his merit, but because of the merits of his forefathers.

A question frequently asked is why the expression is phrased "God of Abraham, God of Isaac, God of Jacob," rather than "God of Abraham, Isaac, and Jacob." Apparently there is a mystical or kabbalistic reason; however, many logical reasons have been given. Isaac Nissim, Sefardic chief rabbi of Israel (1955-1972) explained simply that the wording follows the Torah text in Exodus 3:6

and 3:15.[10] Another rabbi, Meir Eisenstadt, author of *Panim Me'irot,* also alludes to a kabbalistic meaning, but explains that David said to Solomon, "Know the God of your father and serve Him" (1 Chron. 28:9). Therefore, he said, a man should not believe in God merely because his father did. Each person should arrive at his own conviction that God exists. Each patriarch discovered God for himself and so should every Jew. He will thereby acquire a profounder faith.[11]

After mention of the patriarchs, God is referred to as "great, mighty, and revered" (Deut. 10:17). The Rabbis limited the praises at this point to three, following the example of Moses. They felt that expanding the list of adjectives would still not do justice to the Almighty. The Talmud[12] tells of a prayer leader, who expanded the praises, and he was reprimanded by R. Chanina, who told him that the example of Moses, who mentioned only three, was ordained by the Men of the Great Synagogue. He said that the qualities of God were unlimited, and an attempt to number them would ultimately fail and would result in a slight to the Almighty.

Although the three patriarchs are mentioned in the opening of the benediction, it closes with mention of Abraham only. That is based on Genesis 12:2, where God promised Abraham: "And I will make of you a great nation, and I will bless you, *and you shall be a blessing.*"

The first benediction is the only complete one in the *Amida.* It alone opens with *baruch* and closes with *baruch.* Although God's Kingship, a necessary element of a *beracha,* is not expressly mentioned, there is the implication in the words "God of Abraham" because he was the first to recognize God's Kingship over the world.[13] The succeeding benedictions comply with the rules for *berachot* by assimilating the first and joining it.[14]

In the second benediction, mention is made of God's powers and benevolence, emphasizing resurrection. God is praised as He Who sustains all living things with love, resurrects the dead, supports the fallen, heals the sick, and liberates those in bondage. In the fall and winter, God's power as the Giver of rain is mentioned in a verse preceding this benediction. The Talmud[15] states that "The day when the rain falls is greater than the day of revival of the dead, since resurrection is reserved for the righteous alone, while rain benefits all men." In another sense, rain in an agricultural society brings sustenance to mankind, and therefore is a matter of life and death. Rain is mentioned in the blessing of resurrection because the Talmud states[16] that God Himself holds the keys to rain, resurrection, and childbirth and does not entrust them to others. Resurrection is mentioned three times in this paragraph for the purpose of countering the sectarians.

The third *beracha* focuses on God's sanctity. The first two benedictions praise God for material and physical gifts; the third elevates the prayer to a spiritual level. It declares that God is holy, His Name is holy, and holy ones praise Him each day.

When the *Amida* is repeated aloud at the Morning, *Musaf,* and *Mincha* Services conducted with a *minyan,* the *Kedusha* prayer is included. The reason is that true sanctification of God can take place only in public. The Torah says: "And I will be sanctified in the midst of the children of Israel" (Lev. 22:32), and the Rabbis concluded that a manifestation of sanctification can take place only in the presence of a *minyan.*[17]

The *Kedusha* recited in the *Amida* differs from the other *Kedushot—Kedusha de-Yotzer* in the *Keri'at Shema,* and the *Kedusha de-Sidra* in *U-Va le-Tziyon.* In the latter two, the sanctification is by the angels, while in the former, it is Israel that is sanctifying God.

There are two basic parts to the *Kedusha* of the *Amida.* First there is the declaration of intention of Israel to extol and sanctify God, just as the angels have done: "We will reverence and sanctify Thee," in the words of Soferim, chapter 16, section 12. Then there is the recitation of the trisagion, "Holy, Holy, Holy" (Isa. 6:3), and the two responses—the first from Ezekiel 3:12,

"Praised be the Glory of the Lord from His Place"; the second from Psalms 146:10, "The Lord shall reign for ever, Thy God, O Zion, unto all generations, Hallelujah."

The essence of the *Kedusha* is that God is most holy, that His Glory and Presence are everywhere, and He is Eternal King. The *Kedusha* recited by Israel is considered superior to that of the heavenly creatures because the angels recite "Holy, Holy Holy" and only one response, while Israel recites two responses.

## Second Section

During the week, the second section consists of thirteen benedictions, which are supplications. The statutory prayers are in the plural form; thus, the worshiper prays for the needs of all Israel. He is encouraged to insert private requests in various benedictions, as will be noted.

The first through sixth of the intermediate benedictions are for general human needs, while the seventh through the twelfth stress Jewish national aspirations. The thirteenth is a summing up and conclusion for the central portion of the *Amida*.

The intermediate blessings are:

1. *Bina* ("Understanding"). The worshiper first asks for wisdom, understanding, and intelligence. The first words are *Ata chonen*, "Thou graciously givest man wisdom." Use of the verb *to be gracious*, rather than *to give*, implies that knowledge is a gift of God. In discussing the order of the blessings, Judah Halevi says in *The Kuzari*[18] that man first prays for wisdom and intelligence so that he may serve God in a way that man can approach the Almighty.[19] The Talmud states:[20] "Great is enlightenment, for it was set at the beginning of the daily requests."

Another reason the supplicatory prayers start with the request for wisdom may be the verse in Psalms 111:10, "The beginning of wisdom is fear of the Lord" (literally the first words in Hebrew may be understood as "The *beginning* is wisdom"). Another basis may be the verse in Proverbs 4:7, "The *beginning* of wisdom is: Get wisdom; Yea, with all thy getting, get understanding."[21]

Rashi at Exodus 31:3 explains *chochma*, "wisdom," as what someone had learned; *bina*, "understanding," as what a man understands in his heart and infers from other things he has learned; *de'a*, "knowledge," as prophetic inspiration. Samson Raphael Hirsch states that *de'a* means true perception; *bina* is insight, logical judgment; and *haskel* is practical wisdom.[22]

2. *Teshuva* ("Repentance"). The worshiper asks God in this *beracha* to cause Jews to return to Him. It is a principle of Judaism that man has free will, and God has no control over man's moral decisions.[23] The worshiper is saying in effect: "Please help us to repent." This benediction follows the one for wisdom, on the theory that once a person has understanding and wisdom, which are gifts of God, he will return to God on his own. The phraseology of Rosh ha-Shana is used here as in the succeeding benedictions, where God is referred to as "our Father" and as "our King." The opening words are based on Lamentations 5:21, "Turn Thou us unto Thee, O Lord."

3. *Selicha* ("Forgiveness"). As a matter of Halacha, this blessing must follow the one on repentance, inasmuch as one of the first steps toward repentance is confession of sin. True repentance consists of these steps: regret for past deeds, resolve to abandon sin and not repeat it in the future, and confession of sin.[24]

This blessing once again uses terminology of the High Holidays. Misdeeds are classified as sins and transgressions. *Chet* usually means an unintentional offense. The concept of the benediction and its close are based on Isaiah 55:7, "Let the wicked forsake his way, and the man of iniquity his thoughts; and let him return unto the Lord, and He will have compassion upon him, and to our God, for He will abundantly pardon."

The intermediate blessings up to this point are of a spiritual nature. The next three deal with material or physical subjects.

4. *Ge'ula* ("Redemption"). Having shown his desire for repentance and having sought God's forgiveness, the worshiper now asks for redemption. Although uttered on behalf of the community of Israel, this prayer refers to rescue from constant troubles besetting the Jews, not for redemption from exile.[25] Halevi says that the sequence of the benedictions is based on the fact that redemption is the consequence and token of forgiveness.[26]

This redemption benediction is in the present tense and refers to a continuing redemption into the future. The redemption blessing at the close of the *Shema* is in the past tense and refers to the Exodus.

The expression "for Thou art a mighty Redeemer" is based on Jeremiah 50:34 ("Their Redeemer is mighty"). The phrase "See our affliction and plead our cause" is from Psalms 119:153-154, but is pluralized.

5. *Refu'a* ("Healing"). This blessing refers primarily to physical healing. Nevertheless the terminology refers to a twofold healing of both body and soul, "Heal us . . . save us for Thou art our praise." The wording is a pluralization of Jeremiah 17:14. It is important to note that, although Jews are encouraged to pray to God for healing, tradition cautions that one should not rely on miracles, but must seek medical assistance.[27]

6. *Birkat ha-Shanim* ("Blessing of the Years"). This is a prayer for prosperity. Still on the theme of material needs, the worshiper prays for his livelihood and that of the community. As befits the early agricultural society of Israel, emphasis is placed on the produce of the land, specifically Eretz Yisrael, and the need for rain in the proper season.

7. *Kibbutz Galuyot* ("Ingathering of the Exiles"). The expression and the concept "Sound the great horn" is from Isaiah 27:13. Rabbi Elie Munk[28] observes that this *beracha* is the dividing point between personal needs of the people and congregational or national concerns. Hereafter the prayers relate to societal necessities.

8. *Birkat ha-Mishpat* ("Blessing of Justice"). The opening words, "Restore our judges as at first and our

counselors as at the beginning," are based on Isaiah 1:26. Of particular significance is the next verse (Isa. 1:27) which states: "Zion shall be redeemed with justice, and they that return of her with righteousness." The first demand of a society is for God's reign of justice. Thereafter come other benefits. The rabbinical perception of society's needs was clear and fundamental.

The Rabbis warned: "The sword comes into the world for the delay of justice, for the perversion of justice, and on account of those who misinterpret the Torah."[29] The blessing, which asks for God's intervention, confirms the necessity for a society based on law, order, and justice.

9. *Birkat ha-Minim* ("Blessing concerning the Sects"). This paragraph denounced those who deviated from traditional belief. Recitation of the benediction was considered an affirmation of a true believer. Many authorities believe that this was the added benediction to the original eighteen, to bring the total to nineteen. Their opinion is based primarily on the statement in Berachot[30] that Samuel the Little, at the direction of Rabban Gamaliel, formulated the benediction concerning the sectarians, i.e., dissident factions, including Judeo-Christian elements. Other scholars[31] explain the passage in Berachot to mean that Samuel the Little merely expanded the existing *beracha* to include the *minim* (sectarians).

In today's Askenazic prayerbook, the benediction refers to slanderers, evildoers, enemies of God, and the arrogant. The Sefardic prayerbook still uses the word *minim*, translated as "apostates." Other versions of the blessing include the words *meshumadim* and *apikorsim* (converts to other faiths and apostates.).

Because the conclusion of the *beracha* speaks of "breaking the enemies [of Israel]" and "humbling the arrogant," there is an indication that the subject of *minim* may have been a later addition to the paragraph.[32] In talmudic times, if the prayer reader did not recite this paragraph in the repetition of the *Amida*, he was removed because of suspicion that he was a sectarian.[33]

The terminology used in the benediction is significant. "Slanderers" refers to those who informed against their fellow Jews to the Roman authorities. Destruction of the "wicked" is not requested, but destruction of "wickedness." That usage is based on Psalm 104:35, which states: "Let sinners cease out of the earth, and let the wicked be no more." Based on a textual variance, the verse was interpreted in the name of Beruriah, wife of Rabbi Meir, to say: "Let *sin* cease out of the earth, and the wicked will be no more."[34]

"Dominion of arrogance" apparently referred to Rome. The expression "breaks the enemies" is based on Isaiah 14:5, "The Lord has broken the staff of the wicked, the scepter of the rulers." "Subdues the arrogant" is apparently from Isaiah 25:5, "Thou didst subdue the noise of strangers."

This paragraph is the only negative, denunciatory portion of the *Amida*. The curses are mentioned in decreasing severity, from being lost, without hope, cut off and uprooted, to being humbled. The curses are in figurative language and do not signify actual physical suffering.

Those who say that this *beracha* is the nineteenth explain, as previously mentioned, that the name of the *Amida* was not changed from *Shemoneh Esreh* ("Eighteen") to "Nineteen" because it was the hope that the need for the paragraph would be eliminated in time, and the *Amida* would return to eighteen blessings.

10. *Tzadikim* ("For the Righteous"). This is a prayer for the righteous *(tzadikim)*, pious *(chasidim)*, elders, remnant of the scribes and proselytes (converts to Judaism) and those who trust in God. Leviticus 19:32-34 speaks of honoring the elderly and the convert to Judaism. Although various categories are mentioned, the benediction ends with praising God as the "support and trust of the righteous" because that is the major theme of the blessing.

The Jerusalem Talmud explains the sequence of this blessing and the preceding ones in this way: "If the exiles are ingathered, and justice is established, then the arrogant will be humbled, and the righteous will rejoice."[35]

11. *Jerusalem.* This benediction asks for the rebuilding of Jerusalem, the return of God's Presence, and restoration of the throne of David. The expression "building Jerusalem" is found in Psalms 147:2: "The Lord buildeth up Jerusalem. He gathereth together the dispersed of Israel."

Some authorities say that this benediction and the following were one blessing, and it was their separation that changed the number of benedictions from eighteen to nineteen. The Jerusalem Talmud states that the benediction of David was included in the benediction of building Jerusalem.[36]

12. *Offspring of David.* This paragraph refers to the coming of the Messiah, a descendant of David, and to the resultant redemption and salvation.

The word *tzemach*—meaning "shoot," literally, and "offspring," figuratively—is associated with King David and messianic hopes in the book of Jeremiah. The first mention is in 23:5, where it is said: "Behold, days will come, saith the Lord, that I will raise unto David a righteous offspring, and he shall reign as king and prosper, and shall execute justice and righteousness in the land." The second mention is in 33:15, where it is said: "In those days, and at that time, I will cause an offspring of righteousness to grow up unto David, and he shall execute justice and righteousness in the land." The expression "horn of salvation" is found in 2 Samuel 22:3 and in Psalms 18:3.

The request for re-establishment of the Davidic kingdom was originally part of the benediction on rebuilding Jerusalem as mentioned earlier. It was not a separate part of the *Amida*, according to texts found in the Cairo Geniza. It became a distinct *beracha* in talmudic times in Babylon.[37]

13. *Petition for Acceptance of Prayer.* This is the concluding section of the intermediate prayers. It sums up the requests of the worshiper, and asks God to hear the prayers of Israel.

The expression "hear our voice" is found in Numbers 20:16 and Deuteronomy 26:7. The benediction "Who hearkenest to prayer" is mentioned in Yoma 70a, as one of the blessings recited by the high priest on Yom Kippur.

## Closing Benedictions

The next three are the concluding benedictions, traditionally referred to as the blessings of thanksgiving, although they contain elements of petition.

17. *Avoda* ("Restoration of Sacrificial System"). The prayer is known as *Retzeh,* meaning "accept" or "desire." It is an ancient prayer and was recited in Temple days during the sacrificial service. The priests would pray that the offerings be accepted by God.[38] After the destruction, the prayer was altered to petition for acceptance of Israel and its worship and for restoration of the sacrificial system of the Temple.

In reciting the prayer, some join the phrase *ishei Yisra'el* to the preceding *li-devir beitecha,* and some to the succeeding word *u-tefilatam,* placing a pause after *beitecha.* In the former version, the meaning would be: "And restore the worship service to the sanctuary of Thine Temple and the fire offerings. And their prayers mayest Thou willingly in love accept." The second version would be: "And restore the worship service to the sanctuary of Thine Temple. And the fire offerings and their prayers mayest Thou willingly in love accept." The Gaon of Wilna preferred the former version.[39]

The Conservative movement's *Sabbath and Festival Prayer Book* omits reference to the sacrificial system, i.e., the fire offerings, because it does not favor their restoration. It interprets the term *worship* to mean prayer only.[40]

18. *Hoda'a* ("Thanksgiving"). The *Modim* prayer is one of gratitude and expresses appreciation to God for the miracles of daily living. It was recited in Temple times.[41] The Talmud states that the *Avoda* and Thanksgiving prayers were the same.[42]

The word *modim* from the root *y.d.y.* may mean "thank," "confess," or "agree." Rashi says that *hoda'a* is an expression of confession and faith.[43] The word *hoda'a* is the Targum's translation for *hishtachava* ("bowing") in 2 Samuel 16:4. For that reason, the worshiper bows his head and bends the knee when reciting *Modim*. In modern prayerbooks, the phrase *Modim anachnu lach* is variously translated:

Hertz PB—"We give thanks unto Thee" (page 151).
Birnbaum Daily PB—"We ever thank Thee" (page 92).
Hirsch PB—"We acknowledge Thee that Thou are the Lord" (page 66).
Silverman PB—"We thankfully acknowledge Thee" (page 32).

For those who translate *Modim* as acknowledgment, and not thanks, the later phrase *nodeh lecha* is translated as referring to thanksgiving.

In support of the position that *Modim* means an acknowledgment or affirmation of belief, it is observed that in the Talmud, the *Modim* prayer is aligned with the *Shema* in a particular statement dealing with the practices of apostates. One must not say *"Modim, Modim,"* or *"Shema, Shema,"* for it would indicate a duality of the Almighty.[44] From that statement, it may be deduced that *Modim*, like the *Shema*, refers to declaration of God's Unity.

The phrase *"Modim anachnu lach"* is found in 1 Chronicles 29:13. The expression "Merciful One, Thy lovingkindness never ceases" is based on Lamentations 3:22.

Thanksgiving was considered by the Rabbis as the highest level of prayer. They said that, although many sacrifices and prayers would be eliminated in the future, the song of thanksgiving would endure forever.[45] The beauty of the *Modim* prayer is that it expresses appreciation for God's provision of seemingly routine items. For the truly grateful, nothing is taken for granted.

19. *Sim Shalom* ("Grant Peace," Blessing of the Priests). This final benediction, "Grant Peace," correlates with the phraseology of the Priestly Benediction in Numbers 6:24-26, which ends with the word *peace*. Hirsch explains that *Sim Shalom* details the elements of *shalom* mentioned by the priests in their benediction.[46]

The final three blessings of the *Amida* form a unit. The progression is service, thanksgiving, and peace. After the sacrificial service, the thanksgiving prayer was said. Leviticus 9:22 records that Aaron blessed the people after offering the sacrifices. *Sim Shalom*, which follows, carries on the theme of the priestly blessing. The Rabbis also ordained that every important prayer end with a mention of peace.[47]

Because of its relationship to the *Birkat Kohanim*, (Priestly Benediction), *Sim Shalom* is recited in the Ashkenazic ritual only when the priests could utter their blessing, at the Morning and *Musaf* Services. It was then that the priests pronounced the blessing in ancient times. Nowadays, outside Israel, it is Ashkenazic practice that the priests bless the congregation only on holidays not falling on the Sabbath. On other occasions, the threefold blessing is mentioned in narrative form in the Reader's repetition.

The priests were not permitted to bless the people at *Mincha* (Afternoon Service) for fear they might have imbibed intoxicating liquor, which would have disqualified them.[48] The Ashkenazim recite *Sim Shalom* as the final *Amida* blessing only when the Priestly Benediction might be said. That would include *Mincha* on fast days, when there was no fear that the priests would have imbibed alcohol. Sefardim recite *Sim Shalom* at all services. Ashkenazim substitute *Shalom Rav* ("Abundant Peace") at *Mincha* on nonfast days and at *Ma'ariv* (Evening Service).

In order to insert a more universal outlook in the prayer, the Conservative prayerbook has adopted a usage of Rav Sa'adia's *siddur,* and says, *Sim shalom ba'olam* ("Grant peace in the world").[49]

## Conclusion of Amida

With the recitation of *Sim Shalom,* the *Amida* proper is ended. The Talmud states[50] that at the end of the *Amida,* one should say: "Let the words of my mouth be acceptable to Thee" (Ps. 19:15). The usual reason advanced is that David uttered the verse in Psalm 19, and worshipers therefore recite it after the Eighteen Blessings. The Sefardim recite it immediately after *Sim Shalom* and repeat it after *Elohai Netzor* ("O Lord, guard my tongue"). Askenazim usually say it only in the latter case.

It was customary to add private supplications after the *Amida.* R. Joshua ben Levi said that, although the rule was that a man asked for his needs in *Shomea Tefila* ("Who hearkenest unto prayer"), he may add something after the *Amida,* even an order of confession.[51] Sefardim do recite a short confession after the *Amida.*

Approximately eleven examples of private prayers are set forth in the Talmud, Berachot 16b-17a. That of Mar bar Ravina was selected by Ashkenazim. It commences: "O Lord, guard my tongue from evil." The prayer asks that God guard one's speech from vile expressions, slander, and falsehood, and open his heart to Torah. It is a personal prayer and expresses the hope that just as the worshiper has purified his speech to recite the *Amida,* so shall he continue on that high level in his daily communications with his fellowmen.

Thereafter, *Oseh Shalom* is recited. It is based in part on Job 25:2, "He makes peace in high places." The verse was first mentioned in *Machzor Vitry,* where the custom of pacing backwards was described. Before reciting the verse, the worshiper takes three steps back, bows to the left, right, and center, as though taking leave of one's teacher[52] or exiting from the presence of royalty.[53] The backward steps commence with the left foot.

The Sefardim end the complete *Amida* here. The Ashkenazim add *Yehi Ratzon* ("May it be Thy will . . . that the Temple be rebuilt"), based on Mishna Avot 5:20. The Talmud[54] denounces as ill-mannered one who immediately retraces his steps, the apparent reasoning being that it may show dissatisfaction with the prayer. It may be that *Yehi Ratzon* was added to cause the worshiper to pause a moment or two before returning to his place in accord with the edict of the Rabbis. The usual custom is to retrace the three steps in public prayer, when the Reader reaches *Kedusha* in his repetition. The recitation of *Yehi Ratzon* also acknowledges the relationship between prayer and the sacrificial system, the former being a substitute for the latter, according to one opinion.[55]

## Repetition of the Amida

During the Morning, *Musaf,* and Afternoon Services, after the congregation has completed the *Amida* silently, the Reader repeats it aloud, when there is a *minyan.* The Reader as *Sheliach Tzibur* ("Representative of the Community") originally repeated the *Amida* aloud for the benefit of those who were unable to articulate the prayers. In ancient times, there were no readily accessible prayerbooks. The liturgy had to be committed to memory. For those who were not conversant with the prayers, the response of *Amen* to the recitation of the blessings by the Reader was deemed to be personal utterance of the prayers.[56] The same concept governs the repetition in more modern times, inasmuch as some congregants are unable to read the prayerbook.

Repetition of the *Amida* serves a purpose even for those who do know how to pray. It cures any accidental omissions by individuals.[57] In modern times, some have advocated the elimination of the silent *Amida*, making a recitation aloud suffice. Rabbi David Hoffman opposed such a practice because it prevented those who wished to concentrate in silent prayer from so doing; it prevented insertion of private petitions; and based on the original reason for the petition, it stigmatized every worshiper as being unlearned.[58]

During the repetition with a *minyan*, certain prayers are added, such as *Kedusha* (Sanctification); *Modim* of the Rabbis (Acknowledgment and Thanksgiving); and *Birkat Kohanim* (The Priestly Benediction).[59]

At the start of the third benediction, the Reader requests the congregation to join in extolling and sanctifying God. This is known as the *Kedusha da-Amida*. Unlike the *Kedusha* in the *Shema* benedictions, which was known as *Kedusha di-Yeshiva* ("Sitting *Kedusha*") or *Kedusha de-Yotzer,* the *Amida Kedusha* is not a narration of what the angels say, but a declaration of sanctification[60] by the congregation, and therefore requires a *minyan*.[61] The *Kedusha* of the *Amida* was probably first introduced in Babylon and was added later in Palestine. It was recited only on Sabbaths and festivals at the Morning Service until geonic times. It then became customary for daily and *Mincha* services.[62] On Sabbath and festival mornings, Ashkenazim in particular expand the *Kedusha* beyond the three key verses.

When the Reader reaches the eighteenth blessing and recites *Modim,* the congregation rises, bows, and recites its own version, known as *Modim de-Rabbanan* (*Modim* of the Rabbis), because it is collection of verses suggested by various sages.[63] Abudraham explains the congregation's supplementary recitation as necessary because gratitude must be expressed directly and personally, not through a messenger.

The final addition is The Priestly Benediction. In the Temple worship, the priests would ascend a platform, the *duchan* (from which comes the expression *duchanen,* "to recite the priests' blessing"), and bless the people after the offering of the sacrifice and recitation of

*Retzeh.*[64] In Israel today, the priests bless the congregation daily. Outside Israel, the blessing is recited on holidays. At other times, the benediction is said in narrative form by the Reader. As the Reader recites each of the three verses of the benediction, the congregation responds, *Ken yehi ratzon* ("So may it be His will"). *Amen* is considered inappropriate because the Reader is not blessing the people, but only narrating. When the priests pronounce the benediction, it is proper to say *Amen* after each verse.[65]

## Supplements and Modifications

At various times and seasons, the *Amida* is supplemented and certain terminology is changed.

### Ten Days of Penitence

From Rosh ha-Shana through the conclusion of Yom Kippur, the penitential days, certain additions and modifications are made to express the sentiments of the period.
1. Immediately prior to the close of the first benediction, "Remember us unto life, O King . . ." is added.[66]
2. Immediately prior to the second benediction, "Who is like unto Thee, Father of Mercy . . ." is added.[67]
3. The third benediction is altered to conclude with "the holy King," rather than "the holy God."[68]
4. The eleventh benediction is altered to conclude with "the King of Judgment," rather than "the King Who lovest righteousness and judgment." The change is not grammatical Hebrew, but the expression is sanctioned by long usage.[69]
5. In the eighteenth benediction (of thanksgiving) the declaration is inserted: "O inscribe all the children of Thy covenant for a good life."[70]
6. In the nineteenth and final benediction, the conclusion is altered with the preface, "In the book of life,

blessing...," and ends with "Blessed art Thou... Who makest peace."[71]

## Rainy Season

Commencing with the Reader's repetition of the *Musaf* prayer on Shemini Atzeret (eighth day of Sukkot), when a special prayer for rain is chanted, God's power with regard to rain is mentioned in the second benediction with the words, "Who causes the wind to blow and the rain to fall." This insertion continues until the first day of Passover. That statement is not itself a prayer for rain, but merely mentions it.[72] The Talmud states[73]: "The power of rain should be mentioned in the prayer for resurrection of the dead [second benediction]; rain should be prayed for in connection with the prayer for a prosperous year [ninth benediction]."

Rain in an agricultural society like Israel's was vital. Its mention in the second benediction, which enumerates God's powers, thus appropriately places it on a level with the resurrection of the dead. The Talmud in Ta'anit[74] cites the dictum of R. Jochanan that "three keys the Holy One, blessed be He, has retained in His own hands and has not entrusted to the hand of any messenger, namely, the key of rain, the key of childbirth, and the key of resurrection of the dead." Rain is first mentioned on Shemini Atzeret because it was a tradition that, on the Feast of Tabernacles, the world is judged whether it will have rain.[75]

In the winter, shortly before the rainy season, an express prayer for rain is included in the ninth benediction for sustenance. The standard wording, "Give blessing upon the face of the earth" is altered to read, "Give dew and rain upon the face of the earth." This formula is recited until the first day of Passover. The changed form is said starting the evening of December 4 for worshipers in the diaspora. It is calculated as the sixtieth day after the autumnal equinox (about September 22 or 23). It is one of the rare instances when a Jewish observance is governed by the solar calendar alone, rather than by the lunar.[76] In Israel, the prayer for rain is inserted commencing with the evening prayer of the seventh day of Cheshvan, about two weeks after Shemini Atzeret.

## Torah Festivals and New Moon

Whenever a *Musaf* prayer is recited on a weekday, such as the New Moon or the intermediate days of Passover and Sukkot (falling on either a weekday or Sabbath), a special prayer is inserted in the *Retzeh* benediction.[77] That prayer is known as *Ya'aleh ve-Yavo* ("May our remembrance rise . . . and be accepted before Thee"). The prayer is hinted at as the New Moon prayer in the Talmud,[78] but not by its name. It is mentioned by name in Soferim.[79] Rashi says[80] that this prayer is a petition for mercy for Israel and Jerusalem and for restoration of the Temple service and the daily offerings. Its emphasis is on the future. The Jerusalem Talmud states[81] that whatever is directed to the future, like *Ya'aleh ve-Yavo,* is recited in the benediction of the Temple service, and whatever refers to the past, like *Al ha-Nisim* (see below) is recited in the Thanksgiving blessing. *Ya'aleh ve-Yavo* is apparently based on Numbers 10:10, which says, "Also on the day of your gladness and in your appointed seasons, you shall blow the trumpets over your burnt offerings, and over the sacrifices of your peace offerings. And they shall be to you for a memorial before your God." The recitation of the prayer is therefore a memorial of the offerings on their established days and for that reason was inserted in the *Avoda* benediction.

## Chanuka and Purim

The *Al ha-Nisim* ("For the miracles") passage is inserted in the Thanksgiving benediction (the eighteenth on weekdays) on Chanuka and Purim.[82] *Al ha-Nisim* is the introduction for both holidays and is followed by a specific prayer for the particular day. It is interesting to note that in the prayer for Chanuka, no mention is made expressly of the cruse of oil. According to the prayer, the miracle of Chanuka was that through God's help, the few defeated the many, the weak defeated the strong, and so on.

## Public Fast Days

The individual recites *Anenu* ("Answer us, O Lord, answer us on this day of our fast") in the sixteenth benediction immediately prior to the conclusion. The Reader in his repetition inserts that prayer as a separate benediction between the seventh and the eighth and concludes: "Praised art Thou... Who answereth in time of trouble."[83]

In addition, on Tish'a be-Av, all insert the prayer *Nachem* ("Comfort") in the fourteenth benediction during the Afternoon Service and alter its ending to "Praised art Thou... Who comfortest Zion and rebuildest Jerusalem."[84]

## Private Petitions

The Rabbis cautioned against making prayers fixed and routine. They encouraged the insertion of fresh material, such as private supplications, as long as the essential structure of the *Amida* was maintained.[85] In the eighth benediction for healing, a prayer for a particular sick person may be included.[86] In some prayerbooks, a brief confession of sin or a prayer for sustenance may be added to the sixteenth benediction, "Who hearkenest to prayer."[87] The prayer for sustenance approximates a similar one found in the Hertz Prayer Book.[88]

As previously mentioned, it is appropriate to include private prayers at the close of the *Amida* in "O my Lord, guard my tongue."

## Shortened Amida

The Talmud provides for an abridged form of the *Amida*.[89] The first three benedictions are recited, then the abridgment of the central blessings, known as *Havinenu*, and then the final three. It was the opinion of R. Joshua that all that was necessary to recite at any time was the shortened version;[90] however, the current view is that it is to be said only in case of illness or emergency. Because the *Amida* has structural variations on Saturday night (inclusion of *Havdala* in the fourth blessing) and during winter (prayer for rain in the ninth blessing) the abridgment cannot be used at those times. Rashi explains that the abridgment includes the essence of all the central blessings.[91]

# 10.
# MANNER AND MODE OF PRAYER

SINCE PRAYER IS COMMUNICATION with the Almighty, special forms of etiquette are observed while at worship. The development of those forms reveals the attitude and respect the Jewish people have toward God.

## Position

Position is one of those forms. In modern times, there are three basic positions: standing, sitting, and falling on the face. Tradition states that they were learned from Moses. Standing—"And I stood at the mountain" (Deut. 10:10); sitting—"And I sat at the mountain" (Deut. 9:9); falling on the face—"And I fell down before the Lord" (Deut. 9:18,25).

Standing is usually reserved for the more important prayers, for putting on the *talit* and *tefilin,* and for recitation of *Baruch she-Amar,* Psalm of Thanksgiving, *Va-Yevarech David, Az Yashir, Yishtabach, Kaddish, Kedusha,* the *Shemoneh Esreh*[1] (which is also known as the "standing prayer"[2]), *Ve-Hu Rachum* on Mondays and

Thursdays, and *Aleinu*. Much depends on local custom. At all other prayers, including the *Shema*, one may sit. Falling on the face is limited to *Tachanun*, "And David said to God,"[3] when recited in the presence of a scroll of the Torah. The custom is based on the verse in Joshua, "And Joshua . . . fell to the earth upon his face before the Ark of the Lord" (7:6). The *Shemoneh Esreh* must be recited standing, based on Deuteronomy 10:8, which says, "to stand before God to serve Him."

The Talmud states that, while praying the *Shemoneh Esreh* and the *Kedusha*, one must place his feet together as though they were one, so as to emulate the angels.[4] When one is ill or traveling and unable to stand, the *Amida* may be recited in some other position. It is considered disrespectful to pray flat on one's back. If possible, one should sit up or turn to one side if required to pray while ill.[5]

Although the *Shema* is an important part of the service, one need not stand during its recitation. It may be said standing, sitting, or walking inasmuch as the Torah specifically provides in the *Shema* that "these words" shall be spoken of "when you sit in your house, when you walk by the way, when you lie down and when you rise up" (Deut. 6:7). If recited while walking, the first verse, "Hear, O Israel," must be said while standing still so as to maintain a proper sense of devotion.[6]

Falling on the face *(nefilat apayim)* is limited, as previously mentioned, to recitation of *Tachanun* in the presence of the Torah.[7] Then one cradles his face in the crook of the left arm, unless wearing *tefilin*, in which case the right arm is used. That position is mentioned in Leviticus 9:24 and Numbers 14:5.[8]

In ancient times, Jews kneeled and prostrated the whole body to show humility, but those positions have been abandoned almost entirely because they were primarily reserved for use in the ancient Temple service. In modern times, these positions have been avoided because they have been adopted by some non-Jews. Today kneeling and prostration are restricted to brief moments on Rosh ha-Shana and Yom Kippur.[9]

The Talmud states that when one recites the *Amida,* one should direct his eyes downward and his heart heavenward, place his arms folded over his heart, and stand as a servant before his master with awe and respect.[10] Rava folded his hands and prayed like a servant before his master, indicating he stood still.[11] Rabbi Akiba, however, moved about while praying, and the Talmud records that when he prayed by himself, he could be left in one corner and found in another because of his bowing and prostrations.[12]

## Bowing and Bending the Knees

Bowing the head and bending the knees are frequent gestures. At *Barechu,* before the *Shema,* one bows the head and bends the knees. One does likewise several times during recitation of the *Amida.* It is done at the first benediction, beginning and end. The custom is to bow the head at *baruch,* bend the knees at *ata,* and resume a straight position at the mention of God.[13] At *Modim,* the Thanksgiving benediction, one bows the head and bends the knees, and finally at the benediction following, "Thy Name is Good...."[14]

One also bows the head and bends the knees in reciting *Aleinu* at the close of the service upon reading the words, "And we bend the knee, bow down and give thanks," and as in other instances, one assumes an erect position at the mention of God.

At the close of the *Amida* and the *Kaddish,* one steps back three paces at reciting *Oseh Shalom* ("He Who makes peace on high") and bows from the waist to the left, right, and center.[15] Of special ethical interest is the statement in the Talmud that the higher one's position in Jewish life, the more incumbent it was upon him to show his humility. The king was required to kneel throughout the *Amida;* the high priest bowed at each benediction; an ordinary person bowed only at the first and next to last benedictions, as explained above.[16] The Bible notes that King Solomon prayed on his knees (1 Kgs. 8:54).

## Steps Forward and Back

Recitation of the *Amida* incorporates certain royal court customs. Before starting the prayer, the worshiper takes three steps backward and then forward as though entering the presence of an earthly king.[17] On concluding the *Amida,* at *Oseh Shalom,* he steps three paces backward, starting with the left foot, as though leaving the presence of royalty. One must not retrace those steps immediately inasmuch as it is considered disrespectful. For this reason, one waits until he completes the section, "May it be Thy Will . . ." or, if praying with a *minyan,* until the leader reaches the *Kedusha* in his repetition. The custom is mentioned in the Talmud Yoma 53b.[18]

Another reason given for the pacing is that it is reminiscent of a practice of the priests during the sacrificial ceremonies, when they approached and left the altar in the Temple.[19]

## Swaying

Swaying during prayer is a much-beloved Jewish practice. It is affectionately known in Yiddish as *shoklen* (literally, "shaking"). There are dissenting opinions to the custom. One view previously mentioned is that the worshiper must stand as a servant before his master[20] thus indicating a motionless stance.[21] The view followed by most traditional Jews is that swaying adds to concentration, to emotion, and to fervor in prayer. Its origins are varied:

1. One possible origin was the practice of Rabbi Akiba, mentioned previously.[22]
2. Another is based on the verse describing the giving of the Torah: "And all the people perceived the thunderings and the lightnings, and the sound of the *shofar,* and the mountain smoking; and when the people saw it, they trembled and stood afar off" (Exod. 20:15).

3. A third is based on the verse, "All my bones shall say: "Lord, who is like unto Thee . . ." (Ps. 35:10).[23]

4. *The Kuzari*, Part Two, discusses swaying when reading the Torah. The reasoning might well apply to prayer. In answer to a question of the king as to why Jews move to and fro when reading the Bible, the rabbi says:

> As it often happened that many persons read at the same time, it was possible that ten or more read from one volume. This is the reason why our books are so large. Each of them was obliged to bend down in his turn in order to read a passage, and to turn back again. This resulted in a continual bending and sitting up, the book lying on the ground. This was one reason. Then it became a habit through constant seeing, observing and imitating. . . .[24]

The Magen Avraham stated that one may choose to sway or not based upon whichever mode aided his concentration in prayer.[25] One custom permits swaying front to back, but not side to side, because the latter displays an arrogant attitude.[26] Chasidism popularized *shoklen* in modern times. Some swayed violently, and even turned somersaults.[27]

## *Rising on the Toes*

When reciting the *Kedusha* (trisagion—"Holy, Holy, Holy") at the Reader's repetition, one rises on his toes at each mention of the word *kadosh* ("holy"). The purpose is to emulate the angels who, according to tradition, also recited a form of *Kedusha*. The Midrash Tanchuma, Leviticus, *Tzav*, cites Isaiah 6:2 as the source. The verse says: "Above Him stood the seraphim, each one had six wings; with two he covered his face, and with two he covered his legs, and with two he did fly." The following verse (6:3) is the first part of *Kedusha*: "Holy, Holy, Holy is the Lord of Hosts; the whole earth is full of His glory."

Based on the expression, "and with two he did fly," the Rabbis established that one should lift his heels as though trying to reach the essence of God, and then lower them. The Ba'er Heitev states that one should raise his heels at the succeeding verses also, such as *Baruch kevod* and *Yimloch*.[28]

## Modulation of Voice

A classic selection from the Talmud on recitation of prayers states that many customs are derived from the story of Hannah in 1 Samuel 1:10, *et seq.*[29] Rabbi Hamnuna said:

> How many important laws can be learned from the verses relating to Hannah? "Now Hannah, she spoke in her heart"—from this we learn that one who prays must direct his heart. "Only her lips moved"—from this we learn that he who prays must frame the words distinctly with his lips. "But her voice could not be heard"— from this, it is forbidden to raise one's voice in the *Tefila*. "Therefore Eli thought she had been drunk"—from this, that a drunken person is forbidden to recite the *Tefila*....

One who prays must do so in a properly modulated voice. He must pronounce the words, but is forbidden to shout. One interpretation of the word *Shema* ("Hear") is that the one who recites the *Shema* paragraphs[30] must "let his ears hear what his mouth speaks."[31] A person who shouts his prayers is considered to be one of little faith because he believes that otherwise God will not hear him.[32] The Rabbis stated that praying in a loud voice was a heathen practice: "The heathen cries aloud to his god, but he does not hear him. The Jew prays in a whisper and the Holy One gives ear to his prayer."[33] Of course, the prayer leader is permitted to raise his voice so as to be heard by the congregation.[34]

One who answers *Amen* to a benediction should not raise his voice above that of the one reciting the blessing, based on the verse, "Magnify the Lord with me, and let us exalt His Name together" (Ps. 34:4).[35]

Maimonides said:

The voice should not be raised during the recital of the *Amida*, nor should [the prayer] be offered silently in thought alone. The words should be pronounced with the lips, but softly, and yet be audible to the speaker's ears. The worshiper should not permit his voice to be heard by others, unless he is sick, or is unable to concentrate his attention without reading aloud. He may not, however, do so at public worship so that the congregants shall not be disturbed by his loud praying.[36]

It is customary to recite the first verse of the *Shema* ("Hear, O Israel") out loud and to prolong the recitation of the word *echad* ("one"), so that it is certain that the *dalet* is pronounced correctly and is not distorted.[37] Another reason for prolonging the word *echad* was to allow the worshiper to concentrate on declaring God's Kingship in all six directions.[38]

## Other Acts and Gestures

It has long been customary for Jews to show their affection for religious symbols and artifacts by kissing them. The kissing and touching of ritual objects are also a means of making one aware of the *mitzvot* as one performs them.[39] Some instances are as follows:

1. *Tzitzit*. At the recitation of *Baruch she-Amar*,[40] one holds the two front fringes in his hand, kisses them and releases them at the close of the benediction.[41]

During the reading of the *Shema*, one holds all four *tzitziyot*. They are gathered at the recitation of "O bring us in peace from the four corners of the earth" in the *Ahava Rabba* prayer.[42] The gathering is probably done at that point because of the appropriateness of the verse and because it would disturb one's *kavana* to do so during the actual recitation of the *Shema*. The fringes are kissed each time the word *tzitzit* is said, again at the word *emet*, and then kissed and released at *nechemadim la-ad* ("and desirable forever").[43] When reciting "And you shall look upon them," the fringes are held up to view or pressed to the eyes.[44]

2. *Tefilin.* It is customary to kiss the *tefilin* when putting them on or taking them off;[45] and to touch one of the straps of the head *tefilin* to the containers and to kiss it when reciting the following: (a) The benedictions "Who girds Israel with might" and "Who crowns Israel with glory."[46] (b) The verses "Let the heavens rejoice and let the earth be glad" in *Hodu*[47] and "Thou openest Thy hand and satisfiest every living thing with favor" in *Ashrei,*[48] during reading of the *Shema* when *tefilin* are referred to.[49]

3. Covering the head with the *talit.* Many pious Jews cover their heads with the *talit* at various parts of the service, particularly during the recitation of the *Shema* and the *Amida.* One reason is that one thereby eliminates distraction and improves concentration. Another is based on a rule that one must cover his head during recital of the *Amida.*[50] This is interpreted to mean something more than a *kippa* or *yarmulka.* There is a requirement of *ituf* ("wrapping").

The Talmud states that at times Rabbi Kahana put on an upper garment and covered his head with it and prayed.[51] The priests always cover their heads when reciting the Priestly Benediction. It was considered a worthy act because it was also said that God drew His robe over Himself and enwrapped Himself like a prayer leader.[52]

The *Zohar* in Deuteronomy *Va-Etchanan*[53] says that when a man stands in prayer, he should keep his feet together and cover his head as one who stands before a king, and he should shade his eyes so as not to look at the *Shechina.*

4. Recital of first verse of the *Shema.* In addition to the previously mentioned custom of prolonging the word *echad,* it is the traditional practice to close one's eyes and cover them with one hand, while reciting the first verse, *"Shema Yisra'el"* ("Hear, O Israel"). The purpose is to aid in concentration because the recitation constitutes an affirmation of God's Unity. The custom was derived from that of Rabbi Judah the Prince, of whom

the Talmud said, "He passed his hand over his face and accepted the yoke of the Heavenly Kingdom."[54]

5. Beating the heart. When reciting a prayer of confession, it is customary to strike one's heart with the right fist. The rite is based on the belief that the heart was the seat of all thought and action and therefore the source of sinful conduct.[55] On Saturday nights and days when *Tachanun* is not said, the custom is not practiced because those are not times for confession of sins.[56]

6. Opening the hand. When reciting the verse, "Thou openest Thy hand and satisfiest every living thing with favor," in *Ashrei*[57], it is customary to open one hand or both and turn the palm upwards.

7. *Tzedaka*. The Jew is always obligated to give charity. On weekdays at each service, the charity box is either passed around or is placed in a conspicuous place so that everyone can contribute something for the upkeep of the synagogue or for the poor. Rabbi Eliezer would give a coin to the poor before reciting the *Tefila*, based upon the verse in Psalm 17:15: "As for me, I shall behold Thy face in righteousness," the word *righteousness* being interpreted as "charity."[58] Maimonides mentions that the great sages gave a coin to charity before reciting their prayers.[59] It was the custom of Rabbi Isaac Luria to drop coins in the charity box during the recital of "And David blessed the Lord in the presence of all the congregation,"[60] when he reached the words "riches and honor come of Thee and Thou rulest over all."[61]

# 11.

# DRESS AND CEREMONIAL ACCOUTERMENTS

## *Proper Dress*

A person about to pray must be properly attired. Maimonides stated that before praying one should arrange his clothing so as to make a proper appearance, for it is written: "Worship the Lord in the beauty of holiness" (Ps. 29:2).[1] The quotation refers to the talmudic account of R. Judah, who would dress up before he prayed.[2]

Maimonides further stated that one should not pray in sweaty clothes, nor bareheaded, nor barefooted in societies where it was deemed proper to wear shoes in the presence of important personages.[3] At the site of the Holy Temple, for example, it was considered a lack of respect to wear shoes.[4] Particularly when reciting the *Shema* and the *Amida*, one had to be properly clothed. While he might recite the *Shema* clothed from the waist down, he must cover the top of his body for the *Amida*.[5]

A story was told of R. Simon bar Yochai and his son, who, when sentenced to death by the Romans, hid in a cave for twelve years. They stripped off their clothes and sat in sand up to their necks. When the time for prayer arrived, they dressed, covering themselves, and prayed. Thereafter, they removed their garments so they would not wear out.[6]

## Headcovering

Covering of the head by Jewish men, particularly during worship, is now an almost universal practice. Even Reform temples, which at one time discouraged or forbade headcovering, have now made the practice optional. Today young Jews, not necessarily Orthodox, wear a *kippa*, cap, in the streets as a symbol of Jewish affiliation.

Headcovering is not directly ordained in the Torah. R. Solomon Luria (16th century), in an oft-quoted responsum,[7] stated that, since he knew of no authority against the layman's praying bareheaded, he would overrule the prohibition if the great scholars would support him. He made it clear that otherwise he would not reject or challenge the widely accepted practice of praying with the head covered.

Orthodox men wear a headcovering at all times, except for some who go bareheaded when among non-Jews. Conservative Jewish men wear a *kippa* at least when praying, studying Torah, or performing a religious rite.

Origins of the practice are not certain. Some of the reasons advanced are as follows:

1. Among mideastern peoples, covering the head and removing footwear were signs of respect and an indication of participation in holy activity. Moses was told to remove his shoes when on holy ground (Exod. 3:5). In the Holy Temple, the priests wore headgear (Exod. 28:4,39-

40), but there was no provision for shoes or sandals in their prescribed attire (Exodus 28, generally).

Moslems still remove their shoes before entering their holy places to pray. In some societies, on the other hand, the wearing of a hat was considered a sign of formality.[8]

2. Covering the head was in the tradition of the *kohanim*, the priests. As previously mentioned, the high priest in the Temple wore a *mitznefet*, or linen turban with a gold plate (Exod. 28:36-39; Lev. 16:4). The under-priests wore a *migba'at*, which was wrapped around the head, but was not as elaborate (Lev. 8:13).

Just as the priests wore headcoverings as they entered upon the service of God in the Temple (Exod. 28:4), so also did the lay Jew cover his head as he entered upon service of God day by day. Jews were to act like priests: "And you shall be unto me a kingdom of priests and a holy people" (Exod. 19:6).

3. Covering the head developed as a particularly Jewish way of showing piety, modesty, and respect for God.

On discussing modest behavior, the Talmud relates that R. Joshua ben Levi said: One may not walk four cubits with upright (i.e., haughty) stature. R. Huna, the son of R. Joshua, would not walk four cubits with a bare head, and said: "The *Shechina* is above my head."[9] The implication was that to do otherwise was an indication of arrogance and, so to speak, a trespass on God's domain.[10]

A story was told that Rabina was sitting before R. Jeremiah of Difti, when a man passed by without a headcovering. R. Jeremiah remarked: "How impudent is that man."[11]

Nachman ben Isaac's mother would not let him go bareheaded. She said: "Cover your head so that the fear of Heaven may be upon you."[12] It was said that the mitre of the high priest atones for arrogance.[13] The Mechilta on Exodus 14:8, which reads, "And the children of Israel went out [of Egypt] with a high hand," commented that it meant "bareheaded."

Originally headcovering was probably limited to scholars,[14] important persons, and married men.[15] The Talmud states[16] that R. Kahana was a great man and needed a scarf for his head.

The concept of headcovering as a sign of modesty is shown in a statement in the *Zohar*,[17] where it is stated that he who prays should cover his head and eyes so as not to see the *Shechina*.[18] It thus became a custom to pull the *talit* over the head and eyes when reciting the *Amida*.[19]

## Meaning of Headcovering

What does covering the head mean? In ancient times, it meant a scarf. Today it means wearing a skullcap, a hat, or covering the head with a *talit*.

It has been the practice of religious Jews in modern times to wear a skullcap at home, when eating or saying grace,[20] or when studying religious material. When praying the statutory services, it has been the practice of very pious men to wear a hat because it is more formal and decorous.

The *Shulchan Aruch* provides that one should not mention God's Name or enter a synagogue bareheaded.[21] A small cap of straw is considered a covering, but placing one's own hand on one's head is not because both are part of the same body.[22] It was the practice of wise men and their disciples not to pray unless their heads were enwrapped (with a *talit*).[23]

The Mishna Berura[24] states that in our day, at the time of prayer one should wear his regular hat rather than the skullcap, for one does not stand in the presence of important personages in a cap.

In keeping with the concepts expressed above, one should not misread those statements in rabbinic literature that seem to permit going bareheaded. When they speak of bareheadedness, they are talking about a skullcap, not complete bareheadedness.

## Names for Headcovering

Special names usually used for headcoverings are *kippa* and *yarmulka*. *Kippa* is Hebrew for cap. *Yarmulka*, according to some, is derived from a Polish word. It has occurred to the author that, since one purpose of the headcovering was to instill fear of God, the word *yarmulka* could be derived from the Hebrew words *yareh me-Eloka*, meaning "He fears God." *Eloka* is one way religious Jews refer to God in routine conversation so as not to pronounce a holy name. They pronounce the *h* as a *k*.

Gunther Plaut has stated that the word *yarmulka* is derived from the word *armucella*, a head covering of the medieval clergy.[25]

## *Talit*

The *talit*, or prayer shawl, is worn by men at every Morning Service, but one, and by the leader at the morning and other services on Sabbaths and holidays. Specific usages vary according to the custom of the community. In eastern Europe, it was the practice of married men only to wear a *talit* at prayer. Unmarried men would wear a *talit* when called to the Torah, when leading the service, or when performing some other special function. That custom was based on the sequence of verses in Deuteronomy 22:12-13. Verse 12 speaks of *tzitzit*, and verse 13 states: "If a man take a wife. . . ." Thus, it was deduced by the Maharil of Prague that only a married man should wear a *talit*. The Talmud relates that R. Huna asked R. Hamnuna why he wore no scarf, and he replied that he was not married.[26] In some communities, it is the custom for all men and boys to wear a prayer shawl.

Source of the *mitzva* of *tzitzit* is in Numbers 15:37-41. As there stated, the fringes were to be inserted in the four corners of the garments then usually worn. As modes of dress changed, the wearing of four-cornered garments became rare. Thus the *talit*, a large prayer shawl, was designed with four corners to comply with the scriptural ordinance. The *talit* is to be distinguished from the *talit katan*, or *arba kanfot*, which is a small four-cornered garment usually worn under outside garments by observant Jews. That garment is worn all day, while the *talit* is worn only during prayer.

Since the Torah speaks of placing fringes on four-cornered garments only, the Rabbis questioned whether one was required to make a point of wearing some sort of four-cornered garment so as to be able to fulfill the command. The question was debated as follows: Is *tzitzit* an obligation of the garment or of the individual?[27] Maimonides[28] states that *tzitzit* is an obligation of a man who has a four-cornered garment and that, although one is not required to acquire a *talit* so that he can place *tzitzit* on it, a pious man should not exempt himself from this *mitzva*. He urges that one enwrap himself in a garment requiring *tzitzit* in order to fulfill the *mitzva*, particularly at prayer.

Because the Torah says, "And you shall look upon them . . . ," the Rabbis concluded that the wearing of *tzitzit* was limited to daytime, a period of natural light and that women were exempt, as they were from most other time-oriented *mitzvot*. There was a minority view that *tzitzit* was to be worn at night, and therefore women were obligated as well.[29] The *talit* must be large enough to cover one's head and most of the body. That rule is based on Deuteronomy 22:12, which says: "You shall make for yourself twisted cords upon the four corners of your *covering* with which you cover yourself." The modern small *talit* which rests only on the shoulders does not meet that requirement.

An important part of wearing a *talit* is *atifa* ("enwrapping"). The practice of covering the head with the *talit*, at least when donning it, is an essential part of the *mitzva*. The benediction states: "Praised are Thou . . . Who . . . commanded us to enwrap ourselves with the fringes." The formula is found in the Talmud.[30] Worshipers place the *talit* over the head immediately after reciting the *beracha*. Some also cover the head while reciting certain prayers such as *Shema, Amida, Kedusha,* or when called to the Torah. The reasons are various. One is that covering the head at certain important junctures of the service eliminates distractions and aids concentration. Another is that the *tzitzit* is a reminder of all the commandments and by covering one's head and body with the *talit,* one is symbolically enrobing himself with the *mitzvot*. A third is a mystical reason: The *Zohar* says,[31] "When a man stands at prayer, he should keep his feet together and cover his head as one who stands before a king, and he should also cover his eyes so as not to look at the *Shechina,*" which was considered disrespectful.

One performs the *mitzva* as follows: He places the folded *talit* on the right shoulder and examines the four *tzitziyot* to make certain they are intact. Each fringe should have eight strings and five knots. A preliminary prayer is recited. The *talit* is opened and put on. Before the *talit* is actually placed on the head, he should recite the benediction, which must precede the performance of the act. Tosafot[32] comments that the benediction must be recited while one is putting on the *talit* but before completion.

After the head is covered, the four corners are gathered together and thrown over the left shoulder in what is known as the "manner of the Ishmaelites," who covered their heads, but left exposed only the nose and ears.[33] The part of the *talit* covering the head is then removed and placed on the shoulders. A benediction must be recited each time the *talit* is put on, even during a single service, unless it is removed with the intent to replace it.[34]

On days when *tefilin* are worn, the enwrapping in the *talit* precedes putting on the *tefilin*. This is according to the rule that when two *mitzvot* are to be performed at the same time, the one which is more frequent takes precedence. Because the *talit* is also worn on Sabbaths and holidays, when *tefilin* are not worn, the *talit* has priority.[35] There was an early view, supported by Rav Amram, that *tefilin* were to be put on first. Another reason for giving priority to the *talit* is that the *mitzva* of *tzitzit* is equal to all *mitzvot* of the Torah.[36]

The Torah calls for a fringe of blue *(techelet)* on the *tzitzit*. In ancient times that was done with a dye extracted from a particular snail.[37] The identity of the snail has been lost, and the requirement has been eliminated. The only vestige of the practice is the weaving of blue stripes into the body of the *talit*. The Talmud states that the *techelet* (bluish coloring) is not indispensible to the performance of the *mitzva*.[38]

The *talit* is not worn during the Morning Service on Tish'a be-Av as a sign of mourning. It is deferred until the afternoon prayers. A *talit* is worn for the *Kol Nidrei* service on Yom Kippur Eve, so that everyone will be dressed in white. On that occasion, the *talit* is donned before nightfall so that the benediction may be recited.

Whether a woman should wear a *talit* or *tzitzit* has been the subject of debate, as mentioned before. That debate is based on the dispute whether the wearing of *tzitzit* is limited to the daytime.[39] If it is, then *tzitzit* is a time-oriented affirmative *mitzva* from which women are exempt.[40]

Targum Jonathan on Deuteronomy 22:5 states that women should not wear *tefilin* and *tzitzit* because they are male garments. At any rate, the majority view is that *tzitzit* is time prescribed, and women need not wear them.[41] Nevertheless, Maimonides says that a woman may wear *tzitzit*, but should not recite a benediction.[42]

When the *Shema* is recited, the fringes are collected in one's right hand, when reciting the preliminary blessing, *Ahava Rabba*, at the words, "four corners of the earth."[43] They are kissed at each mention of the word *tzitzit*, and again at mention of the words *emet* and *nechemadim la-ad* or *olemei olamin*. When the words "And you shall look upon them" are said, it is customary to gaze upon the fringes or press them against the eyes. This shows affection for the *mitzvot*. At *Baruch she-Amar*, the front two *tzitziyot* are gathered, kissed, and then released at the concluding blessing.[44] The word *talit* means a cover or a cloak in Hebrew, and is derived from the Aramaic word *tolel*, to cover. It is probably related to the Hebrew and Aramaic word *itztala*, meaning a garment,[45] and derived from the Greek word *stole*, origin of the modern word *stole*.

## *Tefilin*

During the weekday Morning Service, men wear the *tefilin* on the arm and the head to comply with the scriptural command, "And you shall bind them for a sign upon your hand, and they shall be for frontlets between your eyes" (Deut. 6:8).

*Tefilin* are to be worn particularly during recitation of the *Shema*, which mentions them. The Talmud states that one who recites the *Shema* without *tefilin* is as one who bears false witness against himself.[46] They are not worn at night, on Sabbaths, nor on holidays. Like the *talit*, they are omitted at the Morning Service on Tish'a be-Av, the fast day commemorating the destruction of the Temple. They are donned at the Afternoon Service.[47] Formerly *tefilin* were worn all day, but the practice was discontinued when Jews circulated among non-Jewish people.

The Talmud explains the reasoning for not wearing *tefilin* at night, or on Sabbaths and holidays. With reference to *tefilin*, Exodus 13:10 states: "And you shall therefore keep this ordinance in its season from day to day." The Talmud states[48] that the word *day* is expressly used to exclude night, and the expression "from day to day" means not all days. Later Exodus 13:16 says: "And it shall be for a sign upon your hand . . . ," which, the Talmud explains, means only on days when you need a sign of God's relationship to Israel. Sabbaths and holidays, days of rest, are signs in themselves. With reference to the Sabbath, Exodus 31:17 states: "It is a sign between Me and the children of Israel forever...."

*Tefilin* are put on when it is light enough to recognize a casual acquaintance four paces away.[49] Each *tefilin* box contains the writing of the four Torah sections dealing with *tefilin:* Exodus 13:1-10—*Kadesh;* Exodus 13:11-16—*Ve-haya ki yevi'acha;* Deuteronomy 6:4-9—*Shema;* and Deuteronomy 11:13-21—*Ve-haya im shamoa.* There are two types of *tefilin:* Rashi, the standard, and Rabbenu Tam,[50] used by very pious persons. The difference is the order of the written sections. Rashi *tefilin* carry the sections as mentioned above, while Rabbenu Tam *tefilin* interchange the third and fourth sections.

Although called the "hand *tefilin*" *(shel yad),* the box is placed on the upper arm. The Talmud explains[51] that the upper arm is meant by the Torah, so that the *tefilin* will be across from the heart. A second reason is that the hand *tefilin* is not to be visible to others because the Torah says: "It shall be sign upon your [singular] hand," meaning a sign for you only. The head *tefilin,* however, must be visible to others.[52] The head *tefilin* is not placed directly between the eyes, as Scripture states, but on the head between the eyes. The Talmud[53] draws an analogy between laws of *tefilin* and laws forbidding certain acts of mourning. Deuteronomy 14:1 states: "... You shall not cut yourselves nor make any baldness between your eyes for the dead." "Between the eyes" in that context means on the head, where one can become bald. The Talmud then reasons that "between the eyes" also means on the head where *tefilin* are concerned.

A righthanded person puts the hand *tefilin* on the left hand, his weaker hand, while a lefthanded person puts it on his right. That is based on interpretation of Exodus 13:16, where the expression "your hand" is spelled in a manner which could mean "your weak hand."[54] *Tefilin* should be put on while one is standing as a sign of respect. The usual Ashkenazic practice is to put the hand *tefilin* on the arm and recite the benediction "to put on *tefilin*"[55] before actually binding it on the arm. That is so the benediction will be recited before the act is performed.[56] The strap of the hand *tefilin* is wrapped around the arm seven times and then around the hand.[57] Thereafter the head *tefilin (shel rosh)* is set in place, and the benediction "concerning the precept of *tefilin*" is recited, followed immediately by the statement, "Blessed be His Name. . . ." This verse is generally said when one has a suspicion about the propriety of reciting a *beracha,*[58] and fears he may have recited a vain blessing.

There was a difference of opinion whether one benediction sufficed for both *tefilin,* or whether each one required a separate blessing. The dispute was resolved by reciting two blessings, but qualifying the second, as previously mentioned.[59] The formulas for the blessings are found in the Talmud and commentaries.[60]

After both *tefilin* are on, the arm strap is then wound three times around the middle finger, and then around the hand as the verses from Hosea 2:21-22 are recited.[61]

When donning *tefilin,* one puts on the hand *tefilin* first, as in the order set forth in Deuteronomy 6:8. However, in removing the *tefilin,* one removes the head *tefilin* first, so that the head *tefilin* is never on alone. That rule is based on the wording of Deuteronomy 6:8, *Ve-hayu—* "And they shall be for frontlets. . . ." The plural usage is interpreted to mean that the head *tefilin* is on only when the hand *tefilin* is worn. The *tefilin* are left on through the usual Morning Service until after the recitation of the *Kedusha* of *U-Va le-Tziyon* ("A redeemer shall come to Zion").[62] Some say that they should be left on until after the Mourner's *Kaddish* following *Aleinu.*[63]

Those who wear Rabbenu Tam *tefilin* follow either of two practices. One is to put on both sets at the same time. The other is to wear the Rashi *tefilin* until after the silent *Amida,* then put on the Rabbenu Tam *tefilin* without a blessing, recite the two sections of the *Shema* mentioning *tefilin,* and complete the service.[64]

On New Moons, *tefilin* are removed after *U-Va le-Tziyon*. On intermediate days of festivals, those wearing *tefilin* remove them before recitation of *Hallel*. As previously mentioned, *tefilin* are not worn on Tish'a be-Av at the Morning Service because they are considered an adornment, and not in keeping with a day of mourning.[65] Lamentations 2:1 states: "He has cast down from heaven unto the earth, the beauty of Israel," which has been interpreted to mean *tefilin*.

## Sash-Gartel

It is the practice of some, primarily Chasidim, to wear around the waist while at prayer a sash or *gartel* made of twined silk.

The Talmud,[66] interpreting the verse in Amos 4:12, "Prepare to meet your God, O Israel," states that it is proper to wear a girdle around the loins when praying. The reason usually given is that there should be a division between the heart and the genitals.

The Tosafists ruled that, because in modern times a belt is worn around the trousers, there was no special need for a girdle at prayer.[67]

Another reason given for the practice is that it recalled the high priest in the Temple, who wore a woven sash over his linen robe (Exod. 28:4,8,39; Exod. 39:29). It was noted that Elijah wore a belt *(ezor)* of leather about his loins (2 Kgs. 1:8). In the Bible in general, the wearing of a sash was symbolic of readiness to engage in activity and do work (e.g., 1 Kgs. 18:46; 2 Kgs. 4:29).

## No Leather Shoes

It is the custom that leather shoes not be worn on Tish'a be-Av as a symbol of mourning.[68] They are not worn on Yom Kippur as a sign of affliction along with fasting, etc.[69]

## Kittel

The *kittel,* or *sargenes,* as it is called in German-speaking countries, is not worn on ordinary weekdays or Sabbaths. It is a white gown, resembling a burial shroud worn during the worship service on Rosh ha-Shana and Yom Kippur by many observant Jews.[70] It is also worn by the head of the household at the Passover Seder, and by many grooms at the wedding ceremony.

The Reader wears it as well when reciting the prayers for dew *(tal)* and rain *(geshem)*[71] and on Hosha'na Rabba, the final day for the sealing of fate for the New Year.[72]

The gown is white, symbolizing purity and the desire for forgiveness at the High Holiday services and at the wedding ceremony. On Passover, it symbolizes freedom and joy.

*Kittel* means gown in Yiddish. It is called *sargenes* especially by German Jews, because it was originally made of serge[73] or in reference to *sarg,* the German word for coffin. The *kittel* also recalls the white garments worn by the high priest when officiating at the Temple (Lev. 16:4).

## The Four Species

The four species are taken during the festival of Sukkot. The *mitzva* is based on the verse in Leviticus 23:40: "On the first day, you shall take to yourselves the fruit of a goodly tree, branches of palm trees, boughs of leafy trees and willows of the brook, and you shall rejoice before the Lord, your God, seven days."

Rabbinic interpretation defines the four species as the citron *(etrog),* the palm branch, myrtle, and willows.[74] The myrtle and willows are bound to the palm branch *(lulav).* The *etrog,* although separate, is held together with the other species as the *mitzva* is performed.[75] The species must be aesthetically pleasing. Dried up, distorted, or otherwise unsightly specimens are not appropriate.[76]

The species are taken on the first seven days of the festival, through Hosha'na Rabba, with the exception of the Sabbath. Use of the species on the first two days of the festival (i.e., the holy days, when no work is performed) is a command of the Torah. Use on the other days is of rabbinic origin.[77]

Rabbinic interpretation of the above-cited verse from Leviticus mandates that one can fulfill the *mitzva* on the first two days of the holiday only with his own four species. Thereafter, he may use a *lulav* and *etrog* belonging to another.[78] One may comply with the Torah's requirement of ownership if he owns a set in partnership with another or others.[79] Technically, a borrowed set is invalid, but one may fulfill the *mitzva* on the first days if another person makes a conditional gift of a *lulav* and *etrog*. The condition is that the set be returned after the *mitzva* has been performed.[80] Some congregations comply with the requirement of ownership by purchasing several sets of the four species for use by members or the public.[81]

The four species are taken in the following manner. The *lulav* is taken in the right hand, and the *etrog* in the left.[82] The *lulav* is held with its spine toward the person performing the *mitzva*. The myrtle *(hadasim)*, which are three in number, should be on the right side, and the willows *(aravot)*, which are two in number, should be on the left. The blessing, or blessings, should be recited while the person is standing and must be recited during the day.[83] Many prefer to recite the blessing in the *Sukka*.

On the first day of the festival, or the first time one makes the *beracha* during the festival, he should recite two benedictions: one over the *mitzva*, i.e., to take the *lulav*, and a second, *She-hecheyanu*, is recited when performing a *mitzva* for the first time.[84] On all other occasions, only the first blessing is said. The benediction refers only to the *lulav* because it is the largest of the species.[85] The blessing over the *mitzva* must be recited before the *mitzva* is performed.[86] Since performance of the command also requires that the four species be held as they grow, the *etrog* is held with the *pitam* (protuberance) facing downward before the blessing is recited.[87] After recitation of the benediction, the *etrog* is turned so that the *pitam* faces upward as it grows, and the *mitzva* is completed. The species are then waved three times in a forward direction and three times back toward the person in each of six directions.[88] According to Ashkenazic custom, the order is east, south, west, north, upward, and downward. If one is praying in a synagogue, whose Ark is at the east wall, he waves front, right, back, left, up, and down.[89]

The four species are held during recitation of the *Hallel* and are again waved upon recitation of the following: *Hodu l-Adonai; Yomar Na; Ana Adonai.* The *lulav* and *etrog* are never waved during mention of God's Name.[90]

While reciting the *Hosha'not* during the procession after *Musaf,* the four species are again held.[91]

## Aravot

On Hosha'na Rabba, the use of the four species is completed, and at the close of the service, one takes a wreath of five willows, not those part of the *lulav,* waves them and strikes them against the floor two or five times. This ritual is a custom instituted by the prophets, and no blessing is recited.[92] The willow ceremony commemorates a ritual followed in the Temple, when willows were used all seven days of the festival.[93]

## Shofar

The *shofar* is sounded as a Torah command on the morning of Rosh ha-Shana, the New Year, as directed in

Numbers 29:1, "... it is a day of blowing the horn unto you."[94] As preparation for the solemn Days of Awe, it is sounded on a voluntary basis from the first day of Elul to, but not including, the eve of Rosh ha-Shana.[95] The purpose is to inspire the congregation to capture the penitential feeling of the approaching holiday season. The *shofar* blasts are often described as the call to repentance.[96]

During Elul, the *shofar* is blown each morning, except on the Sabbath, after the Morning Service, commencing with the first day of the month, which is the second day of the New Moon. The format is *teki'a, shevarim, teru'a, teki'a.* No blessing is recited.[97] On the eve of Rosh ha-Shana, the sounding is omitted to mark a distinction between the mandatory and the voluntary blowing.[98]

A *shofar* may be made of the horn of any *kosher* animal, except those of the bovine family, since that would evoke unhappy memories of the incident of the Golden Calf. Rabbinic tradition also declares that a prosecutor (or antagonist) cannot serve as a defender (or protector). Thus, the horn of a bovine animal which was an instrument of sin cannot be used to summon the Jews to repentance.[99] Ashkenazim customarily use a ram's horn, symbolic of the ram which was sacrificed in place of Isaac (Gen. 22:13), because it evokes memory of a meritorious deed.[100]

On Rosh ha-Shana, the one who sounds the *shofar* recites two benedictions: One relates to the *mitzva* of *shofar*; i.e., to hear the sound of the *shofar*; the second is *Shehecheyanu*, recited upon performance of first-time acts.[101] The one who sounds must have intent to sound the *shofar* for all who may hear the blasts, and those listening must intend to fulfill the *mitzva* through hearing his blowing.[102]

The *shofar* is again sounded during repetition of the *Musaf* prayer.[103] It is forbidden to speak, with the exception of the prayers, from the commencement of the first blasts until the final ones.[104] For that reason, rabbis in traditional synagogues deliver their sermons prior to the first set of blasts.

The *shofar* is never sounded on the Sabbath. If the first day of Rosh ha-Shana occurs on Saturday, the *shofar* blowing is deferred until the following day.[105]

## Havdala (Distinction)

The *Havdala* ceremony closes the Evening Service at the conclusion of the Sabbath and holidays.[106] The *Havdala* prayer is first recited in the fourth benediction of the *Amida*.[107] It is then recited in an extended form. During the ceremony, a cup of wine is used on both the conclusion of the Sabbath and a holiday. On Saturday night, the ceremony ideally makes use of spices and a candle, although they are not absolutely essential. At the conclusion of Yom Kippur, a candle is used, but the spices are omitted.[108]

The Talmud relates[109] that the Men of the Great Assembly instituted for Israel blessings and prayers, sanctifications and *havdalot* (distinctions). At first they inserted it in the *Tefila*. When Israel became richer, they instituted that it should be said over a cup of wine. They later ordained that *Havdala* be said both in the *Amida* and over a cup of wine.[110] Maimonides states that *Havdala* is a Torah commandment. It is part of the *mitzva* to remember the Sabbath both at its conclusion as well as at its inauguration.[111]

*The beverage.* Wine is preferred.[112] However any customary drink of the land can be used, excepting water.[113] The appropriate benediction is recited over the beverage.

*The spices.* One may use any pleasant smelling spices, woods, or plants. Many use the myrtle plant.[114] The purpose is to refresh the soul, which grieves because the Sabbath has concluded and the "extra soul" of that day has departed.[115] The appropriate benediction should be recited depending on whether a spice, wood, or a plant is used.[116]

*The candle.* The candle must have at least two wicks, or two candles must be used. The light is compared to a torch.[117] As one recites the benediction, "Creator of the lights of fire," he holds up his hands to the fire, looks at his fingernails, then turns his palms so as to face him and cups his hands so that a shadow is created. The purpose of lighting the fire is to inaugurate the work week. The glancing at the hands is to make use of the light to distinguish between the fingernails and the flesh and between the shadow and the light.[118] Tradition has it that fire was created at the conclusion of the Sabbath when God gave Adam two stones to rub together to spark a fire.[119]

A mnemonic device for remembering the order of the ritual is *YaVNeH: Yayin*—wine; *Vesamim*—spices; *Ner*—candle; *Havdala*—blessings of distinctions.[120]

Many communities have various customs associated with the wine of *Havdala*, such as rubbing some over the eyes, or touching the pockets, or pouring some out, all connected with symbols of blessing for the coming week.[121]

*Havdala* may be recited through Tuesday night, but after Saturday night, the spices and candle are not used.[122]

## 12.

## BENEDICTIONS (BERACHOT)

ONE OF THE BASIC FORMULAS of Jewish worship is the benediction, the *beracha*, so-called because it commences with the word *baruch* and consists of a blessing or praise of God. *Baruch* is commonly translated as "blessed." Some believe this translation is presumptuous because it conveys the thought that God is in need of man's blessings. They translate the word as "praised," thus denoting that God is the object of man's praises. This concept is subject to the continuing objection that humble man still acts arrogantly if he believes that God needs his praises.[1]

Commentators have avoided the problem by interpreting the concept of *beracha* in various ways. Samson Raphael Hirsch wrote that the phrase *Baruch ata Adonai* ("Praised art Thou, O God") is a pledge of obedience to God.[2] Jacob Emden (1697-1776) stated that the word *baruch* is not an adjective, but a noun, like *rachum* ("merciful") and means that God is the source of all blessings.[3] Rashba (Rabbi Solomon ibn Adret, 1235-1310) said that mortal man is not blessing God, but is acknowledging His sovereignty. He stated that a *beracha* is a prayer that God be blessed by all mankind; that all men should acknowledge His rule.[4]

The word *baruch* is related to the word *berech* ("knee"), which in turn is apparently related to *bereicha,* a water well, from which a weary person drank, while on his knees. That derivation discloses a kinship between the word *beracha* ("blessing") and the concept of obeisance, respect, and submission. In reciting a *beracha,* a Jew is addressing himself to God as the One to Whom homage is due.

*Berachot* ("blessings") are so basic to Jewish life because the Talmud states[5] that one is forbidden to enjoy any of the pleasures of the world without first reciting praise to God. It is through God's love and goodness that these pleasures are made available to man, according to the reasoning of the Rabbis. In this sense, blessing means thanks.[6]

The Talmud elsewhere cites the dictum of Rabbi Meir that one is required to recite one hundred *berachot* each day.[7] The positive effect of following that rule is that the Jew must constantly seek out activity that justifies recitation of a benediction.

Maimonides stated that just as one recites a benediction before deriving pleasure, one recites a benediction over every *mitzva* before he performs it, the purpose being always to remember God.[8] He classifies benedictions as being of three kinds: (1) benedictions over deriving pleasure or benefit; (2) benedictions over performance of *mitzvot;* and (3) benedictions for thanksgiving.[9]

The format (or *matbea*—mintage—the expression used in rabbinic literature) of the benediction was established by the Men of the Great Assembly.[10] The Talmud records that Rav was of the opinion that every *beracha* must contain the name of God, e.g., it must state: "Praised art Thou, O Lord"; while Rabbi Jochanan (whose view prevailed) held that every benediction must also mention the attribute of God's Kingship, e.g., it must state: "Praised art Thou, O Lord, King of the universe *(melech ha-olam).*[11]

One may not deviate from the format *(matbea)* of a particular benediction. It was said that "he who changes the format established by the Rabbis has not fulfilled his obligation [with respect to the benediction]."[12] There are three formats or styles of benedictions established by the Rabbis:

1. *The short form.* "Praised art Thou, O Lord, our God, King of the universe, Who . . . (e.g., brings forth food from the earth)"; or "Praised art Thou . . . , Who hast sanctified us in His commandments and commanded us . . . (e.g., to put on *tefilin*)"—the formula before performing a *mitzva.*

2. *The long form.* "Praised art Thou, O Lord, our God, King of the universe," then the intervening material is inserted and the benediction concludes, "Praised art Thou, O Lord, Who. . . ." Examples are the *Kiddush* on Sabbath and holiday evenings and the first benediction before the *Shema* in the Morning and Evening Services.

3. *The benediction joined to its neighbor (beracha ha-semucha la-chavertah).* This type of blessing ends with the words, "Praised art Thou, O Lord. . . ." Examples are the second benedictions before the *Shema* at the Morning and Evening Services, and *Yishtabach* at the end of *Pesukei de-Zimra.*

The second benediction before the morning *Shema* starts *Ahava Rabba* ("With abounding love") and ends "Praised art Thou, O Lord, Who chose His people Israel with love." Because the benediction does not mention God's Kingship *(melech ha-olam),* it does not, standing alone, conform to the established format of a *beracha.* By its juxtaposition to the first benediction *(Yotzer Or),* it assimilates the Kingship element from it. *Yishtabach* likewise does not mention God's Kingship *(melech ha-olam),* but the Rabbis associate it with *Baruch she-Amar,* the first benediction of *Pesukei de-Zimra.* For that reason, *Pesukei de-Zimra* is considered as one lengthy *beracha,* and it is forbidden to interrupt during the entire recitation.

An unusual application of this rule is found in the *Amida*. All of the benedictions are cast in the form "Praised art Thou, O Lord...." Not even the first benediction mentions God's Kingship expressly with the formula *melech ha-olam*. The Rabbis explained that, because the very first blessing starts with the words, "Praised art Thou, O Lord, our God, and God of our fathers, God of Abraham, ...," Kingship is implied in the words, "God of Abraham," since he was the first to recognize God's Kingship over the world.[13] The succeeding blessings are then associated with the first one.

Although the format of the benediction was fixed in talmudic times, it existed in some form in the Bible. The formula, "Praised art Thou, O Lord, teach me Thine statutes," is found in Psalms 119:12; the expression "Praised art Thou, O Lord, God of Israel, our father from eternity to eternity," is found in 1 Chronicles 29:10.

No benediction is recited over a ritual performed as a custom, for example, taking the willow branches on Hosha'na Rabba.[14] Sefardim for that reason do not recite a blessing over the Half *Hallel* on the New Moon, inasmuch as that recitation is ordained by custom only. Ashkenazim, however, recite a blessing.[15]

As previously mentioned, the benediction must precede the enjoyment or derivation of benefit. Where the benediction is associated with performance of a *mitzva*, the recitation of the *beracha* must precede the act.[16] There are some exceptions. One is the ritual washing of the hands and immersion in a ritual bath. Since one may not always be in a state of cleanliness before washing the hands or immersing oneself, the blessing is deferred in all cases. (Immersion of a convert presents another legal issue.[17]) With reference to washing the hands, one view of Tosafot states that the actual *mitzva* is completed with the drying of the hands, and because the blessing is said before drying, the blessing does precede the act.[18]

Another apparent exception is the lighting of the Sabbath candles. As a general rule, once the woman recites the blessing over the Sabbath lights, she has accepted the obligation of rest and is forbidden to light the candles. She therefore first lights the candles and covers her eyes to postpone the act of lighting (so to speak) until she has recited the blessing. Some however say that one may recite the blessing and then light the candles with the understanding that by recitation of the blessing, she has not yet accepted Sabbath rest.[19]

There are some commandments over which no benediction is recited. The reason is not always clear or uniform. Some commandments may be performed at any and all times, and therefore a *beracha* is not appropriate. Examples are the giving of charity and all negative *mitzvot*.[20] Other commandments involve the cooperation of another person, which may not be forthcoming, resulting in a *beracha le-vatala*, a vain blessing. An example is the giving of charity. The other person may not accept.[21] The foregoing is a sub-rule under a general rule that one does not recite a blessing over anticipated performance of a *mitzva*, if he is not certain that he will be able to perform the *mitzva*.[22]

Some *mitzvot* may involve misfortune of others, and it is considered inappropriate to recite a blessing. Examples are again the giving of charity and visiting the sick. The Talmud states that one does not say a *beracha* on suffering or divine punishments.[23] Another category is a commandment that even non-Jews are expected to perform, such as giving charity, helping others, and visiting the sick.[24]

No blessing is required over a commandment that has some other benediction connected with it. An example is recitation of the *Shema*. The preceding benedictions are considered by some as valid preliminary blessings. No blessing is recited for either a *mitzva* or an act involving a violation of the law, e.g., returning a stolen article or eating forbidden foods.[25]

A benediction, when recited, has as one of its functions to fix the intent to perform the *mitzva*, that is the *kavana*.

In some instances, it is not necessary to recite the *beracha,* but one may listen to another's recitation (intended to include the listener) with the intent to fulfill the *mitzva.* By listening and answering *Amen* one is considered to have recited the blessing. Examples are *Kiddush* and the blowing of the *shofar.*[26]

A special question arises over the wording of a benediction related to a *mitzva* ordained by the Rabbis and not specifically found in the Torah. On lighting the Chanuka candles, one recites the formula, "Who sanctified us in His commandments...," although Chanuka is obviously not mentioned in the Torah. The Talmud[27] explains that the commandment referred to in the blessing is that in Deuteronomy 17:11, which tells Israel to obey the instructions of the sages, who in turn directed the Jews to light the candles.

One interesting feature of the blessing formula with reference to the *mitzvot* is the change from second to third person in the mention of God. The *beracha* starts, "Praised art Thou," and then switches to "Who has sanctified us with His commandments." The usual explanation is that the change in person manifests two aspects of God's relationship to man, the immanent and the transcendental.[28] Solomon ibn Adret commented that the change conveys the thought that, though man can know God through His deeds, His essence cannot be known.[29]

## Amen

Closely related to blessings is the expression *Amen,* which is the usual response in modern times. In Temple times, the response was, "Blessed is the Name of His Glorious Kingdom forever and ever."[30]

When hearing another recite a blessing, one is required to respond *Amen* at the close. When the person reciting the blessing mentions God, it is the practice to say *Baruch Hu u-varuch Shemo* ("Praised is He and praised is His Name"). *Amen* is probably the best known word in any language. It means "I agree" or "I affirm," from a root meaning "be strong, permanent, and stable."[31]

Some say *Amen* is an acronym for *El Melech Ne'eman,* "God Faithful King." *Amen* has three basic functions. It serves as an oath, as statement of acceptance, and as an affirmation. It serves the third function with respect to a blessing. One who says *Amen* after hearing a blessing, states in effect: "That blessing is true, and I believe it."[32] One who says *Amen* after hearing a blessing is considered as though he recited it.[33] That is true even though he did not hear the entire blessing. *Amen* said by one who did not hear the blessing is called *Amen yetoma* ("an orphaned *Amen*").[34]

*Amen* should not be recited more loudly than the original blessing itself. This rule is based on the verse, "Magnify the Lord with me, and let us exult His Name together" (Ps. 34:4).[35]

A person does not usually recite *Amen* after his own blessing. There are exceptions, especially in the Sefardic ritual, where the blessing is at the end of a section of the service. The Sefardim thus say *Amen* at the close of *Yishtabach,*[36] the end of *Pesukei de-Zimra;* at the close of the *Amida,*[37] "Who blesses His people with peace"; and in the grace after meals, "Who rebuilds Jerusalem."[38] That blessing in early times was the close of the grace. Ashkenazim say *Amen* in the latter case only.[39]

# 13.

# THE KADDISH

THE *KADDISH* is probably the best-known portion of the Jewish liturgy. That is so because one form of the *Kaddish* is a mourner's prayer. The *Kaddish* is a doxology—a song of praise to God. Its recitation is a form of sanctification of God's name, and its origins date to the Men of the Great Assembly.
There are four basic forms:
1. *Half Kaddish (Chatzi Kaddish)*—a shortened version.[1] It is recited by the Reader to mark the completion of a part of the worship service.
2. *Full Kaddish (Kaddish Shalem)*, also known as the Reader's *Kaddish*. It is recited by the Reader to mark the completion of an entire service.[2] It contains all of the Mourner's *Kaddish* plus an appropriate verse asking that Israel's prayers be accepted.
3. *Rabbinic Kaddish (Kaddish de-Rabbanan)*. This is recited by mourners after a study period and particularly after aggadic material. It is also said after the study portions that are included in the prayer services. It consists of the Mourner's *Kaddish* with an added paragraph offering prayer for the welfare of scholars and those who study Torah.[3]

4. *Mourner's Kaddish (Kaddish Yatom).* It is recited by mourners on various occasions during the prayer service and after recitations from the book of Psalms.

There are other forms of the *Kaddish,* but they do not form part of the regular prayer liturgy.

The basic *Kaddish* is the Mourner's *Kaddish.* It consists of utterances of praise of God by the recitant, and responses from the congregation, the most frequent being *Amen,* signifying assent and acceptance.[4]

Structure of the *Kaddish* is as follows:

1. The first sentence or paragraph commences: *Yitgadal ve-yitkadash Shemeh Rabba* ("Magnified and sanctified shall be His great Name"). The phrasing is based on Ezekiel 38:23.[5] The congregation responds with *Amen.* The next phrase is "In the world which He created according to His Will, and may He establish His Kingdom...." Sefardim insert after "His Kingdom" *(malchuteh)*—"And may His Salvation flower and may He hasten the coming of His Messiah." The statement is based on the understanding that the *Kaddish* alludes to the messianic era. The full paragraph ends with a call for a response of *Amen.*

2. The congregation continues the response with *Yeheh Shemeh Rabba mevorach le-olam, alemei almaya.* This response is important and significant as will be explained later. Rabbi David de Sola Pool, in his classic work, *The Kaddish,* finds a parallel to this response in Psalms 113:2, which states: "May the Name of the Lord be blessed from this time forth and forever," and in the phrase recited immediately after the *Shema Yisra'el,* "Blessed be His Name whose Glorious Kingdom is forever and ever."[6] Pool points out that the two statements are a close Hebrew version of the Aramaic in the *Kaddish.*[7] He also notes that the Jerusalem Targum, alternate comment to Deuteronomy 6:4, translates *"baruch shem kevod . . ."* as *"Yeheh Shemeh Rabba."*

The response should end with the word *almaya,* according to Pool.[8] Some include the word *yitbarach,* the first word of the following section to make "seven praises."[9]

3. The person reciting continues with *Yitbarach ve-yishtabach....*" After the words *Shemeh de-Kudsha,* the Ashkenazim answer *Berich Hu* ("Blessed is He"), while the Sefardim say *Amen.*

The word *le-ela,* which appears in this section, is doubled during the Ten Days of Penitence. The usual phrasing is *le-ela u-le-ela* ("higher and higher"). Birnbaum suggests that proper Hebrew phrasing would omit the *u-* (meaning "and"), and that the proper expression is *le-ela, le-ela.*[10] The Geniza text shows that in some communities, the word was doubled throughout the year.

Up to this point, the recitation is that of the Half *Kaddish.*

4. The Reader's *Kaddish* at this juncture adds: *Titkabal* ("May the prayers... be favorably accepted").

5. The Rabbinic *Kaddish* instead of No. 4 adds *Al Yisra'el ve-al rabbanan...* ("Unto Israel and unto the Rabbis"). This section compares with the *Yekum Purkan,* another prayer for the scholars, recited on the Sabbath.[11]

6. The Mourner's *Kaddish* after No. 3 continues *Yeheh shelama rabba* ("May there be abundant peace"). The Reader's and the Rabbinic *Kaddish* continue with that sentence after their special insertions.

7. All of the longer *Kaddish* prayers end with the well-known *Oseh shalom bi-meromav* ("He Who makes peace in the high places, may He make peace for us and all Israel, and let us say *Amen*"). It was a later addition to the *Kaddish.*[12]

In the Rabbinic *Kaddish,* this verse has a slight variation. The phrase reads, "He Who makes peace in the high places, may He in His compassion make peace for us...." The expression "He Who makes peace" is from Job 25:2.

Pool points out that numbers 6 and 7 are very close in meaning, No. 6 being in Aramaic and No. 7 being in Hebrew.[12] He also notes that the final section of the *Kaddish* ends with the mention of *shalom* ("peace") as is the custom with many important prayers. *Shalom* means peace, and its root also means completion or end.[13]

The Midrash states:

> Great is peace because all blessings, good [tidings] and consolations which the Holy One, blessed be He, brought upon Israel conclude with [an invocation for] peace; in the reading of the *Shema,* "Who spreads His tabernacle of peace"; in the *Tefila,* "He Who makes peace"; in the Priestly Benediction, "And may He grant you peace."[14]

In keeping with the above thought is the statement of Rabbi Simon ben Halafta that the Holy One found no vessel to hold Israel's blessings excepting peace, for it is written: "The Lord will give strength to His people, the Lord will bless His people with peace" (Ps. 29:11).[15]

The name *Kaddish* is first used and the prayer is first mentioned as a part of the service in Tractate Soferim, dated to the 8th century.[16] The prayer was originally a closing prayer to an aggadic discourse. In support of that contention, Pool cites the following texts:

1. Raba asks: Upon what does the world exist? On the *Kedusha de-Sidra* (the prayer *U-Va le-Tziyon,* "And a Redeemer shall come to Zion") and on the response *Yeheh Shemeh Rabba* recited after an aggadic discourse.[17]

2. A heavenly echo cried out to Rabbi Jose ben Halafta from a ruin:

> When Israel perform the will of Heaven by gathering in the synagogues and study houses and respond: *"Yeheh Shemeh Rabba mevorach,"* the Holy One, blessed be He, shakes His head and says..., "Happy is the King to Whom such praises are offered in His house."[18]

3. Rabbi Ishmael stated that God rejoices and is exalted in His world "when Israel assemble in the study houses to hear *aggada* from a preacher and respond afterwards, '*Amen, yeheh Shemeh Rabba mevorach!*' "[19]

Pool explained that the preacher usually closed his lecture on a messianic note, and the *Kaddish* picked up that theme.[20] Later the *Kaddish* was recited after a lecture following the seven-day mourning period for a scholar. So as not to cause embarrassment, the recitation of the *Kaddish* was later recited on behalf of all departed, not only scholars. This development tied in with another, the concept of the power of reciting the response *Yeheh Shemeh Rabba mevorach.* Great significance was attached to the response as can be concluded from the talmudic selections quoted above. Pool explained that a reference to God's Name requires a response and thus involves the entire congregation.[21]

The evolution of the *Kaddish* into a mourner's prayer in about the 13th century is most unusual since it contains no direct mention of the dead. Pool attributes the development to a combination of notions. One was the importance of the response, *Yeheh Shemeh Rabba* as related in the Talmud.[22] Rabbi Joshua ben Levi stated that "the evil decree is annulled for him who responds *Amen, Yeheh Shemeh Rabba mevorach* with all his strength."

This correlates with another passage, which states that the recitation of the response by sufferers in Gehinnom procures for them instant relief. The theme continues in the legend about Rabbi Akiba, who taught the son of a man suffering in Gehinnom to say *Kaddish* and *Barechu* to obtain relief from punishment for the boy's father. The legend is found in Kalla Rabbati[23], in Seder Eliyahu Zuta, and in Menorat ha-Ma'or.[24] The versions differ in detail, but an approximate composite is as follows:

> Rabbi Akiba went to a cemetery where he met a man carrying a heavy load on his shoulder. The man was crying and groaning. Rabbi Akiba asked: "Are you a man or a ghost." The man answered: "I am a dead man." Akiba then asked what he did in his lifetime. The man replied that he had done evil deeds and therefore had no rest. Akiba asked whether he had left a son. The man answered that he left behind a pregnant wife. Akiba proceeded to the man's former home and located the wife, who was about to be delivered of a son. He waited, cir-

cumcised him, and when he grew up, took him to the synagogue to join in the worship. Akiba had taught the boy to pray and to recite the *Kaddish* and *Barechu* in public. Later Akiba returned to the cemetery and met the man, who said to him: "May your mind be always at rest because you have set my mind at rest."

The second idea Pool mentions[25] is that recital of prayers by an orphan, who evokes responses from the congregation, had redeeming power for the parent. He said:

> The son best confers saving merit on the father by taking some part in the synagogue service in which he is the mouthpiece of the congregation, so that all may see that he is following in his father's footsteps.

This thought is found in the Talmud, where it is said: "A son confers merit on his father."[26]

Since the *Kaddish* by name is a sanctification of God, it can be recited only in the presence of a *minyan*. The Talmud states that all things dealing with holiness require a quorum of ten adult males.[27]

The *Kaddish* must be recited while standing, as do all prayers that are considered matters of sanctification. It is the custom in many synagogues that all worshipers stand during recitation of the *Kaddish*. Pool finds biblical support for standing while engaged with a holy matter in Judges 3:20: "And Ehud said, 'I have a message from God unto thee.' And he arose out of his seat."[28]

Seder Rav Amram Gaon established a custom of bowing (from the waist) at five points during the recitation: 1. *Yitgadal;* 2. *Ba-agala;* 3. *Yitbarach;* 4. *Shemeh de-Kudsha;* 5. *Oseh shalom*. The five instances correspond to the five names of God mentioned in the Targum to Malachi 1:11.

When reciting the final paragraph (the same which closes the *Amida*) the worshiper steps back three paces, bows to the left, the right, and the center, as mentioned above. The custom is based on the practice followed by one retreating from the presence of his teacher, and it is also reminiscent of the practice of the priests and Levites as they retired from service at the Temple.[29]

Mourners recite the *Kaddish* for eleven months. A full year was considered the proper period of mourning. Because the *Kaddish* was regarded as a prayer of intercession for the departed souls, and twelve months was considered the longest period of suffering in Gehinnom,[30] the recitation was limited to eleven months so as not to cast unworthy reflection on the departed.[31]

The Mourner's *Kaddish* is also recited on the *Yahrzeit* (anniversary of death).

The *Kaddish* is primarily in Aramaic because originally it was recited after a lecture, which was attended by persons who did not understand Hebrew. The Rabbis established that the *Kaddish* be said in translation, the vernacular at the time, so all would understand.[32]

## 14.

## THE TORAH SERVICE

IT HAS OFTEN BEEN SAID that when the Jew prays, he speaks to God, but when the Torah is read, God speaks to the Jew. The reading of the Torah is an integral and essential part of the worship service. To the Jew, study is a mode of worship. A regular reading at public services has nurtured the Jewish people through the ages and has instilled and re-enforced a knowledge of Judaism's basic tenets.

The Torah is read when a *minyan* is present on Mondays, Thursdays, Sabbaths (morning and afternoon), festivals and their intermediate days, New Moons, fast days, Chanuka, and Purim. The Torah is divided into fifty-four *sidrot* (weekly portions), one of which is read each Sabbath, if it does not coincide with a holiday. This is in accord with the Babylonian practice. In ancient Palestine, the Torah reading was completed in a three-year cycle.[1]

On Sabbath afternoons, the first section of the portion for the approaching week is read and that reading is repeated on Monday and Thursday mornings. On other days, the selection is prescribed by rabbinic tradition and consists of readings appropriate to the special day. Interpreting the verse "And they went three days in the wilderness and found no water" (Exod. 15:22) the Mechilta states:

> The allegorists say: "They did not find words of Torah, which are likened to water.... It was because they had been without words of Torah for three days that they became rebellious. It is for this reason that the elders and the prophets instituted the reading from the Torah for the Sabbath and for the second and fifth days of the week."[2]

The Talmud states[3] that Ezra ordained that the Torah be read Sabbath afternoons and on Mondays and Thursdays. Referring to the statement in the Mechilta, the Talmud questions whether the reading on Mondays and Thursdays did not, in fact, precede the time of Ezra. Maimonides explains that Moses instituted the reading on Sabbath mornings and on Mondays and Thursdays, but Ezra established the rule of calling three persons and reading at least ten verses.[4]

It is also explained in the Talmud[5] that the Sabbath afternoon reading was to accommodate shopkeepers, who were busy and unable to attend the weekday readings.

Tosafot explains[6] that Mondays and Thursdays were chosen because Moses ascended and descended Mt. Sinai on those days at the time he received the Ten Commandments, and therefore those were considered special days of favor and grace. An added reason was that Mondays and Thursdays were market days and large numbers of persons came to town, affording the reading a large audience.

The Torah service starts with the opening of the Ark, and the recitation of *Va-yehi bi-nesoa ha-aron*, "And it came to pass, when the Ark moved forward" (Num. 10:35), which Moses and the Israelites used to recite when the camp and the Ark of the Covenant moved. Then follows the verse from Isaiah (2:3) stating his vision that "out of Zion shall the Torah go forth," and then a further verse praising God for His gift of the Torah.[7] The verse from Numbers may well be reminiscent of the ancient practice of keeping the Torah scroll in a movable receptacle outside the sanctuary and bringing it in at the time of reading[8]. Although the verses mentioned above are well known as part of the Ashkenazic rite, the Sefardim recite other selections.

Thereafter most congregations add the prayer *Berich Shemeh* from the *Zohar*,[9] which is supplication. The *Zohar* introduces *Berich Shemeh* as follows: "Rabbi Simon said, When the Torah is taken out to be read before the congregation, the mercy gates of heaven are opened and the attribute of love is stirred up, and each one should then recite the following prayer."

*Berich Shemeh* ("Blessed be the Name") is in Aramaic and asks for God's favor, redemption, long life, and sustenance.[10] It expresses trust in God. It closes: "May it be Thy will to open my heart to the Torah, and to fulfill the wishes of my heart and of the hearts of all Thy people Israel for good, for life, and for peace."

At services other than on Sabbaths and holiday mornings, the leader takes the scroll, faces the Ark and recites *Gadelu l-Adonai iti*,[11] and the worshipers respond with *Lecha Adonai*. The Torah is then placed on the reading table, usually on the *bima*, a central platform in the synagogue. It is unwrapped and prepared for reading. At services on Sabbaths and holidays, the leader recites *Shema Yisra'el*[12] before saying *Gadelu*. On holidays additional prayers are recited before removing the Torah from the Ark.[13]

At services other than on Sabbaths and holiday mornings, the *gabbai*, warden, as he calls up the first person to the Torah, recites the prayer, *Ve-tigaleh* ("And may His Kingdom be revealed"). On Sabbaths and holidays, the recitation is *Ve-ya'azor* ("And may He aid").[14] The reason for the difference is that on Sabbaths and holidays, the *haftara* benedictions refer to the Kingdom of David. On weekdays, there is usually no *haftara*, and *Ve-tigaleh* is an appropriate prayer for the Kingdom of David.[15]

## Torah Service

Since the Torah is read from a raised platform, being called up to the Torah is called an *aliya* ("ascension"). The number of *aliyot* (plural) on a particular day is as follows:

—Monday, Thursday, Sabbath, and Yom Kippur afternoon: three, the minimum.
—Fast days (morning and afternoon), Purim, and Chanuka: three.
—New Moon and intermediate days of Passover and Sukkot: four.
—Festivals and Rosh ha-Shana: five.
—Yom Kippur morning: six.
—Sabbath morning: seven.[16]

The Talmud states[17] that, three being the minimum, each day which has additional *aliyot* has something special about it to justify the increase. On Sabbaths, the final section may be divided into smaller portions and more *aliyot* distributed to honor additional worshipers. This is not permitted on other days because prolonging the reading is considered bothersome to the congregation.[18]

On Sabbaths, holidays, and fast days, a *haftara*, or lesson from the Prophets, is read. On Sabbaths, the person called to read the prophetic lesson is called *maftir* and he is the eighth person. For him, the reader repeats a small portion of the seventh reading.[19] Originally the person called up to read the prophetic selection was not called to the Torah. He merely read the portion from the Prophets. It was later decided that he should be called to the Torah so that it would not appear as a disparagement of the Torah.[20] It was further decided that his *aliya* would be additional, and not one of the seven. Thus reading of the *maftir* consists of repeating a small portion of the seventh *aliya*. Since the *maftir* is added on and is not originally part of the Torah reading, the Half *Kaddish* is recited prior thereto to show that the basic reading has been completed, and the *maftir* is added on.[19]

The present custom is to call to the Torah a Kohen first, a Levite second, and Israelites for the next five.

That practice was followed for the sake of preserving peace in the congregation.[21] In the time of the Talmud, a Kohen was not called up first if there were an Israelite of greater scholarly attainment. This custom was changed, and now the third *aliya* is often reserved for the Israelite scholar. A Kohen or Levite may be called for the seventh *aliya* on Sabbaths or for *maftir.*[22]

If there is no Kohen present, a Levite has next priority. If there is no Levite, an Israelite is called first. If there is a Kohen, but no Levite, the Kohen is called for the first two *aliyot.* In ancient times, women were permitted to be called to the Torah. Whether they were actually called is not clear.[23] This practice has not been followed in modern times by Orthodox Jews. The Conservative and Reform groups, however, do call women.

The reader of the Torah, properly called a *ba'al keri'a,* stands with the Torah scroll at his right to comply with the verse in Deuteronomy 33:2, "At His right hand [was] a fiery law unto them."[24] In olden times, each person read his own portion when called to the Torah. So as not to embarrass those who could not read, the position of Torah reader was established.[25] (Some call the reader *ba'al koreh,* but that term is ungrammatical because *koreh* is a verb, or if used as a noun means "reader" and would be redundant.) In Babylon, a translator *(meturgeman)* stood on the platform to translate the Hebrew reading verse by verse into Aramaic.[26]

It is a custom that two members of the congregation stand at the reading table during the Torah service. The reason is that someone should stand with the reader as an intermediary, based on the statement of Moses at the time of giving the Torah: "I stood between God and you" (Deut. 5:5).[27]

A reading portion may not be less than three verses,[28] and the entire reading may not be less than ten verses, except on Purim, when the number is nine.[29]

The person called up recites a benediction both before and after the reading of his selection. In ancient times, the first person recited the opening benediction, and the last person, the final benediction. Nowadays each person called up recites the two blessings.[30]

One called to the Torah approaches the reading lectern by the shortest route. The place in the scroll is pointed out to him by the reader. He touches the place in the scroll with a corner of his *talit*, kisses the corner and releases it. He then grasps the handles of the scroll holder (known as *atzei chayim*, trees of life) and recites the first blessing. After the reading portion is completed, he touches the place with the *talit*, kisses it and releases it. He again grasps the Torah handles and recites the closing blessing. The custom is to roll the scroll closed while reciting the closing benediction so that it does not appear as though he were reading the benediction from the Torah. He recites the first benediction with the scroll open so as not to delay the service. However, he glances to the side so as not to appear as if reading the blessing from the Torah.[31] The obvious reason is that there should not be even the appearance of extraneous matter being added to the words of the Torah. It is customary to lift the handles while reciting the word *Torah* in the blessings.

After one's portion is concluded, the person called up moves to the right until the following reading is concluded, so as not to appear in a hurry to leave the Torah. (Sefardim leave the platform once their reading has concluded.) For the same reason, he returns to his seat by the longest route. Congregants greet one returning from an *aliya* with *Yishar kochacha*, "May your strength be directed in a straight path." This greeting is usually in Yiddish form, which is *Yasher Koach*. Sefardim say *Chazak u-varuch*, "Be strong and blessed."

After the Torah reading is completed, except on Sabbath afternoon, the Half *Kaddish* is recited. On Sabbath and holiday mornings, the Half *Kaddish* is recited before the *maftir* to signify that it is an addition and not part of the required Torah reading.

When there is a special *maftir* section, not part of the regular weekly Torah portion, a second Torah scroll is taken from the Ark and rolled in advance to the proper place so the service will not be delayed.[32] The second scroll is placed on the lectern at the side of the first scroll while the Half *Kaddish* is recited.

Once the entire reading has been concluded in a scroll, the scroll is opened three columns wide and raised so that the script can be viewed by the congregation, which then recites the verse, "And this is the Torah which Moses placed before the Children of Israel..." (Deut. 4:44; Num. 4:37). Sefardim usually display the script before the Torah is read, a more logical custom. The Torah script must be shown to the congregation, and therefore the *magbiah*, the one who lifts, must turn it to all four directions.[33]

In talmudic times, the person who received the last *aliya* would lift the Torah and roll it. Now the two functions are divided. The one who lifts is not called up to the Torah for a reading, and a second person, the *golel*, rolls the scroll, ties it, and replaces the cover and ornaments. When the Torah is rolled, it should be centered at a seam in order to prevent tearing the script.[34]

## *Return to the Ark*

After the Torah is read, and after the *haftara* reading, if any, the scroll is returned to the Ark. The leader recites the verse from Psalm 148:13, *Yehalelu* ("Let them praise"). The congregation responds with verse 14, "His majesty is above the earth and heavens...." On weekdays, Psalm 24 is recited as the Torah procession returns to the Ark. Psalm 29 is recited on Sabbaths, because the Rabbis considered that psalm to be a Sabbath hymn. The congregation then recites *U-ve-nucho yomar* ("And when it rested he said," Num. 10:36) and other biblical verses extolling the Torah. Finally Lamentations 5:21 is said as the Ark is closed: "Turn Thou us unto Thee, O Lord, and we shall return; renew our days as of old."

## Special Prayers

A special prayer is recited for each person called to the Torah or for lifting or rolling it. The prayer is known as a *Mi she-berach* ("May He Who blessed our forefathers"). One version of the blessing is a prayer for the sick. Another is for naming of a newborn daughter.[35]

Another prayer is that by the father of a Bar Mitzva. He recites the blessing, "Praised be He who had freed me from the responsibility for this child."[36] The meaning relates to the fact that the Bar Mitzva is now of age and is responsible for observing the commandments. Conservative Jews, critical of the negative connotations of the prayer, have substituted the *She-hecheyanu* (blessing of gratitude) which is recited on landmark and joyous occasions to thank the Almighty for having reached the milestone.[37]

A benediction of thanksgiving is recited for deliverance from danger.[38] Although the one who recites it need not be called up to the Torah, this is the usual practice. The blessing must be recited before a *minyan*, and, in large congrogations, where each person affected cannot be called to the Torah, the blessing is recited at some point in the Torah service. The categories of persons who recite the prayer are those who have recovered from serious illness, have journeyed across the sea or a wilderness, who have been released from captivity, or have escaped great danger.[39]

The blessing recited is based on Psalms 107:8,15,21,31-32: "Let them give thanks unto the Lord for His mercy. . . ." It should be recited within three days after delivery from the danger.[40] The formula is "Praised art Thou . . . Who doest good unto the undeserving and Who has dealt kindly with me." The congregation responds: "He Who has shown you kindness, may He deal kindly with you forever."[41]

Memorial prayers, *El Maleh*, are recited on occasion of a *yahrzeit* during the week and on Mondays and Thursdays before the Torah is returned to the Ark.[42]

# NOTES

## Guide to Citations and Notes

Abbreviations have been kept to a minimum. In biblical references, only the books of the Torah are abbreviated, because of frequent citation, as Gen., Exod., Lev., Num. and Deut.

In citing the Mishna, the letter M precedes the name of the tractate, which is followed by the chapter and number of the particular mishna. The Babylonian Talmud references mention only the tractate and the folio designation. References to the Jerusalem, or Palestinian, Talmud carry the letter J before the name of the tractate, followed by chapter, section, or folio designation.

The *Mishneh Torah* of Maimonides is cited as MT, followed by subject matter title, chapter, and paragraph. The *Shulchan Aruch* is cited by part, chapter, and paragraph, e.g. Orach Chayim 24:4. References to Tur specifically say so.

Prayerbook references carry the name of the author followed by PB. *Otzar Dinim u-Minhagim* of J. D. Eisenstein is cited as *ODM*.

Notes ordinarily give a short description of a work and edition, unless that is the only citation of the work. A fuller description is contained in the reference list. A bracketed number, e.g. [7], in a note refers to a prior note in the same chapter.

NOTES

## Notes to Chapter 1: Philosophy of Prayer

1. Yehezkel Kaufmann, *The Religion of Israel*, translated and abridged by Moshe Greenberg (Chicago, 1960), pages 109-110.
2. Berachot 10a.
3. MT Tefila 1:1.
4. Maimonides, *Guide for the Perplexed*, translated by M. Friedlander (New York, 1956), page 386.
5. *The Kuzari*, part 3, paragraph 5, Hirschfeld translation (New York, 1978), pages 139-140.
6. *The Insecurity of Freedom* (Philadelphia, 1966), page 20.
7. Abraham J. Heschel, *Man's Quest for God* (New York, 1954), page 10.
8. Ze'ev W. Falk, *Administration of Justice* (Jerusalem, 1981), page 62, states that the usual term for prayer, *tefila*, was derived from the root *p.l.l.*, meaning "to act as a judge, to assess, to estimate," and that originally a person praying asserted his righteousness and asked God to do justice.
9. Samson Raphael Hirsch, *Nineteen Letters*, translated by Bernard Drachman (New York, 1942), page 130.
10. Samson Raphael Hirsch, *Horeb*, translated by I. Grunfeld (London, 1962), volume 2, page 472.
11. [9], pages 129-130.
12. [4], page 332.
13. [9], pages 127-128.
14. Hertz PB, page 116.
15. Two articles of special interest are found in *The Jewish Library*, Leo Jung, editor (London, 1968): Nathan Isaacs, "Study as a Mode of Worship," volume 1, page 131, and Edwin Collins, "Worship as a Mode of Study," volume 1, page 145.
16. [9], page 131.
17. Bernard M. Casper, *Talks on Jewish Prayer* (Jerusalem, 1963), page 131.
18. Louis Jacobs, *Jewish Prayer* (London, 1962), page 13.
19. M Berachot 9:3.
20. Berachot 60a.
21. Joseph Albo, *Sefer ha-Ikkarim*, translated by Isaac Husik (Philadelphia, 1946), book 4, chapter 16, page 145.
22. [21], book 4, chapter 18, page 160.
23. Rosh ha-Shana 18a.
24. [22], page 165.
25. [21], book 4, chapter 20, page 182.
26. [21], book 4, chapter 24, page 215.
27. [26], page 216.
28. [26], pages 217-218.

29. [26], pages 218-219.
30. [10], volume 2, page 475.
31. [9], pages 129-130. Rabbi Avraham I. Kook, late Ashkenazic chief rabbi of Palestine, wrote that prayer does not undertake to change anything in the Deity, Who is the source of all eternity and is not within the realm of change. But rather the nature of prayer is to elevate the worshiper, though tied to the world, to the Divine heights. Prayer is the cornerstone in the completion of man and his attaining perfection (*Seder Tefila*, with Commentary Olat Re'iya [Jerusalem, 1938-39], volume 1, page 14).
32. [9], pages 130-131.
33. [7], pages 7-8.
34. [7], page 15.
35. [25], "God does not need anybody's service."
36. [18], page 20.
37. [10], volume 2, pages 475,522.
38. [7] page 53.
39. [7], pages 54-55.
40. [7], page 56; also Fritz A. Rothschild, "Conservative Judaism Faces the Need of Change," *Commentary* (November, 1953), pages 447-450.
41. [18], page 3; according to Berachot 7a, God prays: "Be it My will that in My dealings with My children, My [attribute of] mercy overcome My [attribute of] justice."
42. Pesachim 50b.

## Notes to Chapter 2: Prayer as Mitzva

1. MT Tefila 1:1, citing Ta'anit 2b. *Sefer ha-Mitzvot*, Mitzvat Aseh 5.
2. MT Tefila 1:2, 5. The Talmud in Bava Metzi'a 107b interprets Exod. 23:25 to refer to recitation of the *Shema* and the *Amida*.
3. Nachmanides, *Sefer ha-Mitzvot*, Nos. 5,10.
4. Berachot 26b.
5. *ODM*, page 443. Leo Rosten in *The Joys of Yiddish* (New York, 1968), page 95, says the origin may be the word *divine*, as in divine service or worship.
6. Berachot 26b.
7. Berachot 26b, Rashi s.v. *u-fedarim*. It was argued that the two theories were really one basis for threefold prayer. The Rabbis encouraged Jews to follow the practices of the patriarchs, but also wanted their decree to have a Torah basis. They therefore likened the prayer services to the sacrifices that were mandated by the Torah. See also Nachman Kahana, *Mei Menuchot* (Jerusalem, 1981), English edition, Berachot, page 126.
8. Berachot 27b.
9. MT Tefila 1:6.
10. Berachot 26b.
11. Berachot 32b.
12. Songs of Songs Rabba, Soncino translation, page 232.
13. Tanchuma, Gen., *Mi-Ketz*, chap. 43, v. 13, Buber edition, section 11, pages 98a-b.
14. Berachot 32a.
15. Tanchuma, Deut., *Ki Tavo*, chapter 26, verse 1, Buber edition, section 1, page 23a.
16. Israel Abrahams, "Some Rabbinic Ideas on Prayer," in *Studies in Pharisaism and the Gospels*, 2nd series (Cambridge, 1924), page 84.

## Notes on Chapter 3: Structure and Composition of Prayers

1. Berachot 32b; Shabbat 10a (regarding study).
2. J Berachot 1, 3b.
3. Berachot 32b.
4. Mechilta, Lauterbach edition (Philadelphia, 1933), *Be-Shalach*, volume 2, pages 91-92; George Foote Moore, *Judaism in the First Centuries of the Christian Era* (New York, 1971), volume 2, pages 227-228.
5. Berachot 33b.
6. Berachot 33a.
7. J Berachot 5,9b; 6,10b.
8. See, e.g., Berachot 28b-29a,34a.
9. Moore [4], page 226.
10. Avoda Zara 8a; Berachot 16b-17a.
11. There is an interesting midrash in Pesachim 117a, which explains why some psalms begin, "To David, a psalm," and some, "A Psalm of David." When inspiration came first, it was "To David, a psalm." When inspiration was slow in arriving, David began to sing, and then inspiration came. In that case, it was "A Psalm of David." The author has heard creative writers say that inspiration rarely comes spontaneously. It is only after they have set aside time and have begun to write that ideas come to mind.
12. Abraham J. Heschel, *Man's Quest for God* (New York, 1954), pages 30-32.
13. Chaim Grade, *The Yeshiva*, translated into English by Curt Leviant (Indianapolis, 1977), volume 2, page 192.
14. Chapter 7, Nos. 1 and 2.
15. Berachot 13a.
16. Berachot 12b.
17. Sota 32b; Orach Chayim 101:4.
18. Orach Chayim 101:4, Mishna Berura, note 15.
19. Shabbat 40b.
20. Rashi on Num. 8:25 and 9:16. M Arachin 2:3-6; M Shekalim 5:1.
21. M Bikurim 3:3-4.
22. Arachin 11a; M Shevu'ot 2:2.
23. Tosefta, Sota 6:2.
24. Berachot 6a.
25. Megila 32a; Tosafot, s.v. *ve-ha-shoneh*, adds that a tune was an aid to memory.
26. Berachot 57b.
27. Abraham Milgrom, *Jewish Worship* (Philadelphia, 1971), page 29.

28. William Congreve, *The Mourning Bride* (London, 1903), act 1, scene 1.
29. Shabbat 35b. The *chazan* was the overseer or what is referred to today as the *shamash*. M Yoma 7:1, Rashi s.v. *chazan*.
30. M Yoma 7:1.
31. J Berachot 9,12b; Tosefta Megila 4:21.
32. Ta'anit 16a.
33. Orach Chayim 53 expands on the qualifications of the prayer leader.

## Notes to Chapter 4:
## Kavana and Frame of Mind

1. M Berachot 5:1.
2. Berachot 28b.
3. Berachot 31a.
4. Berachot 31a; Eruvin 64a; MT Tefila 4:15.
5. Berachot 32b.
6. Eruvin 65a.
7. Berachot 31a.
8. MT Tefila 4:15.
9. Berachot 27a.
10. Maimonides, *Responsa*, edited by Jehoshua Blau (Jerusalem, 1960), volume 2, pages 379-380.
11. Berachot 31a.
12. Pesachim 114b; Rosh ha-Shana 28b; Berachot 13a.
13. Sukka 39a and Tosafot there, s.v. *over*.
14. MT Chametz u-Matza 6:3.
15. MT Shofar 2:4.
16. [14], Commentary of Maggid Mishneh.
17. Commentary to Berachot 12a.
18. Orach Chayim 98:1.
19. Commentary on Orach Chayim 60.
20. Berachot 13a-b; Orach Chayim 60:5, Mishna Berura, note 11.
21. MT Shema 2:1.
22. Orach Chayim 60:5, note 11.
23. MT Tefila 4:15,16.
24. MT Tefila 10:1.
25. Louis Jacobs, *Hasidic Prayer* (New York, 1975) pages 144-147; J. David Bleich, *Bircas ha-Chammah*, Artscroll Mesorah Series (Brooklyn, 1980), pages 113-116.
26. Gershom G. Scholem, *Major Trends in Jewish Mysticism* (New York, 1965), pages 275-276, and *Kabbalah* (New York, 1974), pages 176-180.
27. Orach Chayim 1:4.
28. *The Kuzari*, Hirschfeld translation (New York, 1978), book 3, paragraph 5, page 139.
29. *Chovot ha-Levavot* 8:3,9.

## Notes to Chapter 5: Place, Time, Community

1. M Zevachim, particularly chapter 5.
2. Two key verses are usually cited: Hosea 14:3, "And we shall render for bullocks, the offering of our lips," and Psalms 141:2, "May my prayer be set forth before Thee as incense." Also Orach Chayim 98:4.
3. Berachot 6a.
4. Berachot 8a. The Talmud relates that when Rabbi Jochanan was told that there were old men in Babylon, he was surprised because it was written in Deut. 11:21, "That your days may be multiplied ... upon the land," meaning the land of Israel and not other lands. They then told him that the people came early and late to the synagogue to pray, and he said: "That is what helps them." Rabbi Joshua b. Levi said to his children: "Come early to the synagogue and leave it late so that you may live long." The same concept is mentioned in Avot de-Rabbi Natan 12,23a.
5. Berachot 8a.
6. Psalms Rabba on Psalm 4.
7. Berachot 28a.
8. Berachot 16a.
9. Cf. the patriarch Isaac, Gen. 24:63. The Rabbis said that he went out to the field to pray (Berachot 26b).
10. Berachot 30a.
11. Berachot 24a,25b; MT Tefila 4:1,8,9.
12. Berachot 10b; MT Tefila 5:4,6.
13. MT Tefila 11:4.
14. Berachot 10b.
15. Cited in Beit Yosef, Orach Chayim 90.
16. Berachot 34b and Rashi, s.v. *chalonot*. The late Chief Rabbi Kook offered a sensitive homiletic rendering of the rule. Prayer of the individual reaches perfection only when the worshiper appreciates and understands his relationship to his fellowman and the outside world. One who prays must be aware of others, and prayer in a windowless closed room isolates him (*Seder Tefila, Olat Re'iya*, volume 1, page 259).
17. Rachel Wischnitzer, *The Architecture of the European Synagogue* (Philadelphia, 1964), pages 14,279.
18. *Zohar* (Mosad Harav Kook, Jerusalem, 1964), Exod., *Pekudei*, page 501; Orach Chayim 90:4. Maimonides, however, in one of his responsa stated that the necessity of windows applied only to a private home, referring to the prayer of Daniel (Maimonides, *Responsa*, Blau edition, No. 216, pages 380-381).
19. Berachot 6b.
20. Berachot 7b.

21. J Berachot 4,8b. MT Tefila 5:6.
22. Berachot 30a.
23. Maimonides, Commentary on the Mishna, Berachot 1:2.
24. Orach Chayim 89:1, Be-ur Halacha. Orach Chayim 58:1 states that the starting time for the *Shema* is at a time one can recognize an acquaintance from a distance of four cubits. See, generally, J. David Bleich, "Daylight Saving Time and Morning Prayer," in *Tradition*, volume 14 (Spring 1974), pages 106-112.
25. M Berachot 1:2.
26. M Berachot 4:1; Orach Chayim 286:1 states that the time is from after *Shacharit* to the end of seven hours, or until the end of daylight.
27. M Berachot 4:1.
28. MT Shema 1:9.
29. Orach Chayim 233:1, Mishna Berura, note 14; Orach Chayim 267:2, Mishna Berura, note 3.
30. Berachot 27b.
31. M Berachot 4:1.
32. Berachot 26a-b; MT Tefila 3:9; Orach Chayim 108:1ff. This practice varies from the rules of the sacrifical system.
33. Hertz PB, pages 138, 140. The source of the latter phrase is from Jeremiah 17:14, where it is in the singular.
34. Avoda Zara 7b.
35. Avoda Zara 8a; Berachot 31a.
36. Hertz PB, pages 140-142,146,154.
37. Berachot 30a.
38. Berachot 12b.
39. M Berachot 4:4; Berachot 29b.
40. Pinchas Shapiro of Koretz, Chasidic rabbi (1725-1790), quoted in Martin Buber, *Tales of the Hasidim* (New York, 1947), volume 1, page 126.
41. Part 3, paragraph 17-19, Hirschfeld translation (Shocken edition, New York, 1978), pages 155-157.
42. [41], page 156.
43. Berachot 8a.
44. Berachot 7b-8a.
45. Berachot 7b.
46. *Sifrei* (Horovitz edition, Jerusalem, 1966), Numbers, *Pinchas*, page 181, section 135.
47. Berachot 6a.
48. Hertz PB, p. xix.
49. *Man's Quest for God* (New York, 1954), page 45.
50. See also Magen Avraham, Orach Chayim 46:1.
51. Berachot 6a.
52. [50], s.v. *u-minayin*. See also Megila 23b.
53. Berachot 21b; Megila 23b; Proverbs 14:28 says, "In the multitude of people is the king's glory," and the Rabbis interpreted the verse to mean that public worship should be well attended.

## Notes to Chapter 6: Preliminary Blessings

1. Orach Chayim 1:1.
2. Hertz PB, pages 8-11.
3. Berachot 60b.
4. Orach Chayim 4:1, Mishna Berura, note 1.
5. Orach Chayim 4:1, Mishna Berura, note 6.
6. Chulin 107a.
7. Berachot 51a, Chulin 107a.
8. Compare Isaiah 63:9; Targum on Ezekiel 3:12.
9. Hirsch PB, page 6.
10. See chapter on Benedictions (*Berachot*); Pesachim 7a, Tosafot s.v. *al ha-tevila*.
11. Berachot 11b.
12. Berachot 11b, s.v. *she-kavar niftar*.
13. Hertz PB, pages 11-16.
14. Responsa No. 64.
15. Hertz PB, page 18.
16. Berachot 60b.
17. Sanhedrin 105b.
18. Berachot 8a.
19. Hertz PB, pages 6-7 and 1004.
20. Berachot 60b.
21. Menachot 43b.
22. J Berachot, chapter 9, mishna 2.
23. Pool, *Book of Prayers* (New York, 1974), page 2.
24. Montefiore and Lowe, *Rabbinic Anthology* (Philadelphia, 1960), pages 507 and 656-658, note 9 (p. 656).
25. Isidore Epstein, *Judaism* (London, 1959), pages 168-169; Berachot 16a, Sukka 25a.
26. Berachot 16b.
27. Hertz PB, pages 27-33.
28. Hertz PB, page 930. See also Yoma 87b.
29. Berachot 13b.
30. Keritot 6a; Yoma 33a; Mishna Zevachim, chapter 5.
31. Beit Yosef, Tur, Orach Chayim 3.
32. Megila 31b.
33. Twersky, *Rabad of Posquires* (Philadelphia, 1980), page 101-102.
34. M Avot 5:23.
35. Hertz PB, page 234.

## Notes to Chapter 7:
## Pesukei de-Zimra

1. M Berachot 5:1.
2. Shabbat 118b.
3. Shabbat 118b.
4. MT Tefila 7:12.
5. Berachot 32a.
6. Berachot 31a, Rashi, s.v. *ela mitoch*. Tosafot, *idem*. rabbanan avdei makes the same point. See also Tur, Orach Chayim 93:2.
7. Berachot 4b.
8. Soferim 17:11.
9. Rif on Berachot 32; Orach Chayim 51:4, Rema.
10. Tur, Orach Chayim 51.
11. *ODM*, pages 52-53.
12. Leviticus Rabba 9:7; Pesikta de-Rav Kahana, piska 9:12.
13. Orach Chayim 51:9, Rema.
14. Psalms, Soncino edition, page 304; *ODM*, page 216.
15. J Shevu'ot 1:8.
16. Berachot 4a.
17. Berachot 32b, Tosafot s.v. *kodem*.
18. Psalms, Soncino edition, page 230.
19. Munk, *World of Prayer* (New York, 1953), volume 1, page 84.
20. Orach Chayim 51, Mishna Berura, note 19, Ba'er Heitev, note 7, quoting Mishnat Chasidim.
21. [20], Ba'er Heitev, note 7.
22. Trachtenberg, *Jewish Magic and Superstition* (New York, 1970), pages 95-97. Munk [19], volume 1, pages 84-85.
23. Pesachim 118a.
24. Zohar, Exodus, Teruma, page 132.
25. Orach Chayim 53:1.
26. Orach Chayim 51:3, 4.

## Notes to Chapter 8: Keri'at Shema

1. MT Tefila 9:1.
2. Orach Chayim 55:1; Soferim 10:7.
3. M Berachot 7:3.
4. Berachot 50a.
5. Berachot 49b.
6. Orach Chayim 57:1, citing the Tur, but Mishna Berura, note 8, states that selection may be recited only when the reader is chanting a tune, but not when he is saying the words.
7. M Berachot 1:4.
8. Elie Munk, *World of Prayer* (New York, 1953), volume 1, pages 107,119. This is also a key formula of Franz Rosenzweig (see *The Star of Redemption* [New York, 1971], pages 112-253).
9. *Kuzari* 3:17, Hirschfeld translation, page 152.
10. [9], pages 153-154.
11. Berachot 11a.
12. Berachot 11b, cf. Berachot 31a, and Tosafot, s.v. *she-ken*.
13. Chagiga 12b; Psalms 104:24.
14. [9].
15. Chagiga 13b-14a.
16. Megila 23a; Berachot.
17. MT Tefila 7:17.
18. Orach Chayim 59:3.
19. R. Asher b. Yechiel, responsum 4:20, quoting from Chagiga 12a, cited in Louis Jacobs, *Theology in the Responsa* (London, 1975), page 81.
20. Berachot 11b, Tosafot, s.v. *ve-rabbanan*.
21. Berachot 12a.
22. Berachot 11b; and Tosafot there, s.v. *she-kavar*; MT Tefila 7:10.
23. Max Kadushin, *Worship and Ethics* (Evanston, Ill., 1964), pages 89-90.
24. Cited in Louis Jacobs [19], page 235. Another possible reason is that the *Keri'at Shema* consists of Torah selections, and the worshiper early on has recited a *Birkat Torah*, a Torah benediction, in the preliminary blessings.
25. R. Levi said that if the *dalet* of *echad* were replaced by a *resh*, the world would be destroyed (Song of Songs Rabba on 5:11, Soncino edition, page 241).
26. Hertz PB, pages 210-211.
27. Commentary on Deut. 5:6.
28. This observation was made by the noted otologist, Victor Goodhill, M.D., a Judaic scholar, during a private study session.
29. Theodore Reik, *Mystery on the Mountain* (New York, 1959), page 168.

30. Berachot 13b.
31. Orach Chayim 61:5.
32. [30].
33. Pesachim 56a, Rashi; [30].
34. [30].
35. Berachot 15a.
36. [30].
37. J Berachot 2:9,4a.
38. Orach Chayim 63:2, Mishna Berura, note 7.
39. Orach Chayim 61:3, Rema.
40. Shabbat 119b.
41. Also Orach Chayim, 61:3.
42. Louis Ginzberg, *Geonica* (New York, 1968, 2nd ed.), volume 1, page 138.
43. Berachot 13a.
44. Ta'anit 16b.
45. Companion to the *Authorised Daily Prayerbook* (London, 1914), pages 50-51.
46. Deut. Rabba 2:36.
47. Pesachim 56a; Gen. Rabba 98:3.
48. [44].
49. M Yoma 6:2.
50. Saul Lieberman, *The Martyrs of Caesarea* (Annuaire de l'Institut de Philologie, Brussels, 1944), volume 7, pages 425-427.
51. [43].
52. MT Keri'at Shema 1:2.
53. J Berachot 2:1,4a.
54. See also Ramban on Deut. 11:13.
55. Berachot 12b. Tosafot, s.v. *bikeshu*, states that the Decalogue is mentioned in the three paragraphs.
56. [21].
57. J Berachot 1:8,3c.
58. Jerusalem, 1953, page 31; [41].
59. Berachot 12a; Rashi, s.v. *she-ne'emer*, and Tosafot, s.v. *emet*.
60. M Tamid 5:1.
61. [59].
62. J Berachot 1:9,3d; also Exodus Rabba on 22:3.
63. Berachot 4b and 9b.
64. Berachot 31a.
65. *Kuzari* 3:17, Hirschfeld translation, page 154.
66. Hans Lewy, editor, *Three Jewish Philosophers* (New York, 1969), page 110.
67. *Tradition*, volume 17 (Spring 1978), page 55.
68. Heinemann and Petuchowski, *Literature of the Synagogue* (New York, 1975), page 15.
69. Berachot 4b, s.v. *zeh ha-sameach*.
70. J Berachot 1:1,2d.

## NOTES

71. "The Architectonics of the Siddur," *Niv ha-Midrashiya* (Winter 1966), pages 71-75.
72. Orach Chayim 66:7-8, and Mishna Berura.
73. Hertz PB, pages 304-314.
74. Hertz PB, pages 304-305.
75. [11].
76. [20].
77. Hertz PB, pages 310-311.
78. Hertz PB, pages 312-313.
79. [21].
80. Berachot 4b, and Tosafot, s.v. *amar Rabbi.*
81. Commentary on Berachot; Tur, Orach Chayim 236.
82. [80].
83. Berachot 27b.
84. [80].
85. Berachot 31a, s.v. *ela mi-toch simcha.*
86. Responsum 14.

## Notes to Chapter 9: Amida

1. MT Tefila 5:1-2.
2. Sota 32b; Berachot 24b.
3. Commentary on Berachot 28b, s.v. *be-Yavneh tikenuhu*.
4. R. Zvi Yehudah, quoted in B.S. Jacobson, *The Weekday Siddur*, English translation (Tel Aviv, 1978), page 167.
5. Berachot 32a; Avoda Zara 7b.
6. MT Tefila 1:5-6.
7. Berachot 9b.
8. Rosh ha-Shana 32a.
9. Merits of the fathers has been referred to as "original virtue" by S. Levy, *Original Virtue and Other Short Studies* (London, 1907), page 47.
10. Louis Jacobs, *Theology in the Responsa* (London, 1975), pages 315-316.
11. [10], pages 186-187. The same concept is found in Martin Buber, *Ten Rungs* (New York, 1947), pages 13-14.
12. Berachot 33b; Megila 25a.
13. Berachot 40b, Tosafot, s.v. *amar Abayei*.
14. Max Kadushin, in *Worship and Ethics* (Evanston, Ill., 1964), page 96, states that the blessings are joined conceptually by the acknowledgment of God's love which is carried over from one *beracha* to the next.
15. Ta'anit 7a.
16. Ta'anit 2a.
17. Berachot 21b; Megila 23b.
18. Chapter 3, part 19, Hirschfeld translation, page 157.
19. See also Megila 17b.
20. Berachot 33a.
21. Compare also Solomon's priority request for understanding, which found favor with God (1 Kgs. 3:5-14).
22. Hirsch PB, page 134.
23. Megila 23b; Berachot 33b.
24. MT Teshuva 2:1-4.
25. Rashi, Megila 17b.
26. [18], page 158.
27. Berachot 60a; Bava Kama 85a.
28. *World of Prayer*, English translation (New York, 1953), volume 1, page 138.
29. M Avot 5:11.
30. 28b-29a; Megila 17b.
31. Heinemann and Petuchowski, *Literature of the Synagogue* (New York, 1975), pages 32-33.

## NOTES

32. Max Kadushin, *Worship and Ethics* (Evanston, Ill., 1964), pages 101-105.
33. Berachot 29a.
34. Berachot 10a; see also comment of Wilna Gaon to Orach Chayim 241. He preferred the phrase "Let evil perish."
35. J. Berachot, 2,4,5a.
36. [35].
37. B.S. Jacobson, *The Weekday Siddur* (Tel Aviv, 1978), pages 173-174,197-198.
38. Yoma 68b; M Tamid 5:1; M Yoma 7:1.
39. Orach Chayim 120, Mishna Berura, note 1; Elie Munk [28], page 150.
40. See Foreword by Robert Gordis, pages ix, 32. Richard Rubenstein questions the omission (*After Auschwitz* [Indianapolis, 1966], page 93).
41. M Yoma 7:1; Yoma 68b, Rashi s.v. *ve-al ha-hoda'a*; M Rosh ha-Shana 4:5.
42. Megila 18a.
43. Sukka 45b.
44. Berachot 33b.
45. Lev. Rabba 9:7.
46. Hirsch PB, page 156.
47. M Tamid 5:1; M Ta'anit 4:1; Berachot 12a.
48. Ta'anit 26b; Orach Chayim 129.
49. Silverman PB, Foreword, page xi.
50. Berachot 4b.
51. Avoda Zara 8a.
52. Yoma 53b.
53. MT Tefila 2:9.
54. [52].
55. Berachot 26b.
56. Rosh ha-Shana 34b; MT Tefila 9:3, 8:9.
57. [56]; Tosafot, Berachot 29b, s.v. *ta'ah ve-lo hizkir*. Kahana, *Mei Menuchot*, English translation (Jerusalem, 1981), pages 132-133.
58. [10], pages 295-296.
59. M Megila 4:3.
60. Soferim 16:12.
61. [17].
62. Louis Ginzberg, *Geonica* (New York, 1968), volume 2, pages 48,52.
63. Sota 40a.
64. M Tamid 5:1.
65. *ODM*, page 22.
66. Hertz PB, pages 132-133.
67. [66], pages 134-135.
68. [66], pages 136-137.

69. [66], pages 142-143.
70. [66], pages 152-153.
71. [66], pages 154-155.
72. M Ta'anit 1:1.
73. Ta'anit 2a.
74. Ta'anit 6b ff.
75. Ta'anit 2a, citing Rosh ha-Shana 16a.
76. Another instance is *Birkat ha-Chama* (Blessing of the Sun).
77. Shabbat 24a.
78. Berachot 29b.
79. Soferim 19:7.
80. [77], s.v. *ha-me'ora ba'avoda*. Also Tosafot, s.v. *be-boneh Yerushalayim*.
81. J Berachot 4:3.
82. Soferim 20:8.
83. Hertz PB, pages 140-141,146-147.
84. Hertz PB, pages 284-285.
85. Berachot 29b; Avoda Zara 8a.
86. Hertz PB, pages 140-141.
87. Hirsch PB, page 144.
88. Pages 238-240.
89. Hertz PB, pages 158-159.
90. M Berachot 4:3.
91. Berachot 29a, s.v. *me'ein kol beracha*.

NOTES

## Notes to Chapter 10: Manner and Mode of Prayer

1. Hertz PB, pages 50-52,60-61,90-104,104-106,212-213,134-137, 130-156.
2. Soferim 16:12.
3. Hertz PB, page 180.
4. Berachot 10b, 17a.
5. Berachot 13b.
6. J Berachot 2, 4a; MT Keri'at Shema 2:3.
7. Orach Chayim 131:2, Rema.
8. Berachot 31a, 34a,b.
9. Orach Chayim 131:1, Isidore Epstein, *Judaism* (London, 1959), pages 175, 179.
10. Yevamot 105b.
11. Shabbat 10a.
12. Berachot 31a.
13. Berachot 14a; Orach Chayim 113:7.
14. Berachot 34a; Orach Chayim 113.
15. Orach Chayim 123:1, 2.
16. Berachot 34a-b, Rashi.
17. Orach Chayim 95:1, Rema.
18. Also Orach Chayim 123:1,2.
19. [18].
20. Yevamot 105b; Shabbat 10a; Orach Chayim 95:2.
21. MT Tefila 5:4.
22. [12].
23. Orach Chayim 48:1, Rema quoting Abudraham.
24. Judah Halevi, *The Kuzari*, part 2, paragraph 80, Hirschfeld translation, page 128.
25. Commentary on Orach Chayim 48:1, note 4.
26. Orach Chayim 48:1 and commentaries.
27. Louis Jacobs, *Hasidic Prayer* (New York, 1975), chapter 5.
28. Orach Chayim 125:2, Magen Avraham; Tanchuma, Lev., *Tzav.*
29. Berachot 31a.
30. Hertz PB, pages 116-117.
31. M Berachot 2:3.
32. Berachot 24b.
33. J Berachot 9, 13a.
34. J Berachot 1, 3b; Orach Chayim 101.
35. Orach Chayim 124.
36. MT Tefila 5:1,9.
37. In the Torah script, the *dalet* in *echad* is oversized so it will not be confused with a *resh*. In Exod. 34:14, the *resh* is oversized to avoid confusion with a *dalet*. R. Levi said that if the *dalet* in *echad* were replaced by a *resh*, the world would be destroyed since

the Unity of God would be negated (Song of Songs Rabba on 5:11, Soncino edition, translation by Maurice Simon, 1951, page 341).
38. Berachot 13b. The Talmud also says that one who prolongs *echad* prolongs his life. Orach Chayim 61:4,5, Rema [26].
39. Orach Chayim 28:1.
40. Hertz PB, pages 50-52.
41. Orach Chayim 51:1, commentaries of Ba'er Heitev and Mishna Berura.
42. Hertz PB, page 116.
43. Orach Chayim 24:1.
44. Orach Chayim 24:4, Mishna Berura.
45. Orach Chayim 28:3.
46. Hertz PB, page 23.
47. Hertz PB, page 55.
48. Hertz PB, page 89.
49. Hertz PB, pages 119,125; Orach Chayim 61:25.
50. Orach Chayim 91.
51. Shabbat 10a.
52. Rosh ha-Shana 17b, referring to Exod. 34:6.
53. *Zohar*, Deuteronomy, *Va-etchanan*, Soncino edition, translation by Maurice Simon and Harry Sperling, volume 5, pages 342-343.
54. Berachot 13b.
55. Ecclesiastes Rabba, chapter 1, verse 16. The Midrash says with reference to chapter 7, verse 2 ("And the living will lay it to his heart"): "And why beat on his heart? To say, 'You are to blame' " (Soncino edition, translation by L. Rabinowitz, pages 46-47). The Magen Avraham cites the foregoing Midrash and the works of R. Isaac Luria to the effect that one should strike his heart with his fist when reciting the confessional (commentary on Orach Chayim 607:3).
56. *ODM*, page 110.
57. Hertz PB, pages 88-89.
58. Bava Batra 10a.
59. MT Matnot Aniyim 10:15; Orach Chayim 92:10.
60. Hertz PB, page 99.
61. *ODM*, page 113; Mishna Berura on Orach Chayim 92:10.

## Notes to Chapter 11:
## Dress and Ceremonial Accouterments

1. MT Tefila 5:5.
2. Berachot 30b.
3. MT Tefila 5:15; Orach Chayim 91:5.
4. M Berachot 9:5.
5. Berachot 24b,25a; MT Keri'at Shema 3:17; Orach Chayim 91, Mishna Berura.
6. Shabbat 33b.
7. Responsum No. 72; also quoted in Simon Hurwitz, *The Responsa of Solomon Luria* (New York, 1938), pages 109-111.
8. Particularly where it was part of a uniform for formal dress. R. Solomon Luria (Maharshal) suggested that Jews were permitted to wear hats at services because the Jewish religion prefers simplicity in the worship of God. [7].
9. Kiddushin 31a.
10. Orach Chayim 2:6.
11. Kiddushin 33a.
12. Shabbat 156b.
13. Zevachim 88b.
14. Nedarim 30b.
15. Kiddushin 29b.
16. Kiddushin 8a.
17. *Zohar*, Deuteronomy, *Va-etchanan*, Soncino edition, volume 5, page 342.
18. Sanhedrin 22a states that one who prays should behave as though the *Shechina* were before him.
19. Orach Chayim 8:2,3, Mishna Berura
20. Cf. Rav Ashi, Berachot 51a.
21. Orach Chayim 91:3.
22. [21], Mishna Berura, note 10.
23. Orach Chayim 91:6.
24. Orach Chayim 91, note 12.
25. W. Gunther Plaut, "The Origin of the Word 'Yarmulke,'" *Hebrew Union College Annual*, 1955, volume 26, pages 567-570. Leo Rosten, *The Joys of Yiddish* (New York, 1968), *Yarmulkah* entry.
26. Kiddushin 29b.
27. Menachot 41a, 42b.
28. MT Tzitzit 3:10-11.
29. Menachot 43a.
30. Berachot 60b.
31. [17].
32. Yevamot 90b.
33. Mo'ed Katan 24a.

34. Menachot 43a; Orach Chayim 8:14, Rema and Mishna Berura.
35. Menachot 43a; Nedarim 25a.
36. Apparently because the *tzitzit* is a reminder of all the commandments.
37. Menachot 42b.
38. Menachot 38a. For a fascinating story about a modern search for the source of the dye, see Abraham Israel Kon, *Prayer* (London, 1971), chapter 12.
39. Menachot 43a.
40. Berachot 20a; M Berachot 3:3.
41. Also Kiddushin 33b, 34a.
42. MT Tzitzit 3:9.
43. Hertz PB, pages 116,117.
44. Orache Chayim 24:2,4; The Rema mentions that kissing the *tzitzit* is a sign of affection for the commandments (Yalkut Shim'oni on Psalms, section 723).
45. Shabbat 128a.
46. Berachot 14b, Tosafot, s.v. *u-maniach tefilin*.
47. Orach Chayim 555:1, Mishna Berura.
48. Menachot 36a.
49. Berachot 9a.
50. Grandson of Rashi, lived c. 1100-1171; *ODM,* page 444.
51. Menachot 37a,b.
52. Menachot 17a.
53. Menachot 37b.
54. Menachot 37a.
55. Hertz PB, pages 48-49.
56. Menachot 35b.
57. Orach Chayim 25:11, Rema and Mishna Berura.
58. Orach Chayim 206.6.
59. Orach Chayim 25:5, Mishna Berura, note 21.
60. Menachot 36a, Rashi and Tosafot, s.v. *lo*.
61. Hertz PB, pages 48-49.
62. Orach Chayim 25:13, Rema.
63. Orach Chayim 25:13, Mishna Berura.
64. Orach Chayim 34:1.
65. Orach Chayim 555:1, Mishna Berura.
66. Shabbat 10a.
67. [66], Tosafot, s.v. *terichuta*; Louis Jacobs, *Hasidic Prayer* (New York, 1975), pages 47-48. Cf. Orach Chayim 91:2.
68. Orach Chayim 554:16-17.
69. Orach Chayim 511:1; Yoma 11a; Shabbat 10a, Tosafot, s.v. *rami puzmaki*.
70. Orach Chayim 610:4, Rema.
71. God's power over rain was frequently associated with His power over life and death (Ta'anit 2a).
72. Orach Chayim 664:1, Magen Avraham.

## NOTES

73. *ODM*, page 364.
74. Sukka 35a.
75. Orach Chayim 651:1,2,11; MT Lulav 7:6.
76. E.g., Sukka 31a and 34b; see M Sukka, chapter 3:1-6.
77. M Sukka 3:12; Orach Chayim 658:1; MT Lulav 7:15, 17.
78. M Sukka 3:13; Orach Chayim 658:3.
79. Orach Chayim 658:7,8,9.
80. Orach Chayim 658:4,5; Kiddushin 6b.
81. Orach Chayim 658:9, Mishna Berura, note 40.
82. Sukka 37b; Orach Chayim 651:3.
83. Orach Chayim 651:5, Rema; Orach Chayim 652:1.
84. Orach Chayim 651:5.
85. Sukka 37b.
86. Orach Chayim 651:5, Mishna Berura, note 24.
87. Orach Chayim 651:2, Mishna Berura, notes 16,17.
88. Orach Chayim 651:8,9.
89. *ODM*, pages 190-191; Orach Chayim 651:10, Mishna Berura, note 57.
90. M Sukka 3:9, Orach Chayim 651:8, Mishna Berura, note 37.
91. Orach Chayim 660:1,2.
92. Orach Chayim 664:2,4, Mishna Berura, note 19.
93. M Sukka 4:3,5.
94. MT Shofar 1:1; Orach Chayim 588:1.
95. Orach Chayim 581:1, Rema. Some start the first day of the New Moon. Orach Chayim 581:1, Mishna Berura, note 3; Orach Chayim 581:3.
96. MT Teshuva 3:4.
97. *ODM*, page 17.
98. Orach Chayim 581:3, Mishna Berura, note 24.
99. Rosh ha-Shana 26a.
100. Orach Chayim 586:1, Mishna Berura, note 2; Rosh ha-Shana 16a. Another reason for use of a ram's horn is that the blowing of the *shofar* on Rosh ha-Shana is by tradition associated with the blowing of a horn to institute the Jubilee Year at the close of Yom Kippur, for which a ram's horn was used (Lev. 25:9; MT Shofar 1:1).
101. Orach Chayim 585:2; MT Shofar 3:10
102. Orach Chayim 589:9; MT Shofar 2:4,5.
103. Orach Chayim 592:1.
104. Orach Chayim 592:3, Mishna Berura, note 11; MT Shofar 3:11.
105. Orach Chayim 588:5; MT Shofar 2:6,8,9,10.
106. Hertz PB, pages 744-748.
107. Hertz PB, pages 278-279; Orach Chayim 294:1
108. Orach Chayim 298:1; Orach Chayim 297:2, Mishna Berura, note 2.
109. Berachot 33a.
110. Berachot 33a, b.

111. MT Shabbat 29:1. If one recites *Havdala* in the *Amida*, the later recitation over the wine is considered a rabbinic edict (Orach Chayim 296:1, Mishna Berura, note 1).
112. MT Shabbat 29:6.
113. Orach Chayim 296:2; Orach Chayim 272:9, Mishna Berura.
114. Orach Chayim 297:4.
115. Orach Chayim 297:1, Mishna Berura, note 2; Ta'anit 27b, on the departure of the "extra soul"; MT Shabbat 29:29. Maimonides says that the soul grieves because the Sabbath has departed and is refreshed with the good aroma.
116. Hertz PB, pages 746-747,988-989; Orach Chayim 297:1, Mishna Berura, note 1.
117. Orach Chayim 298:2.
118. Orach Chayim 298:3, Mishna Berura, notes 9, 10; MT Shabbat 29:25; Berachot 53b. In Pirkei de-Rabbi Eli'ezer (c. 8th century), chapter 20, it is mentioned that Adam stretched his hands to the light, pronounced a blessing and looked at his fingernails.
119. Pesachim 54a.
120. Orach Chayim 296:1.
121. *ODM*, pages 89-90; Isaac Klein, *Guide to Jewish Religious Practice* (New York, 1979), page 74. In Eruvin 65a, it is said that a house where wine is not poured out like water will show no sign of blessing.
122. MT Shabbat 29:4; Tur, Orach Chayim 299.

## Notes to Chapter 12: Benedictions

1. Louis Jacobs, in *Jewish Prayer* (London, 1962), page 20, says that the purpose of the blessings cannot be to fill a need of God, but rather to direct our minds to higher ideals. Albo, in *Sefer ha-Ikkarim* (Philadelphia, 1946), book 4, chapter 20, page 182, says that God does not need anybody's service. He interprets the praises in the worship service as meaning that man thereby acknowledges that all things come from Him and that we have no other source of support outside of Him.
2. Hirsch PB, page 5.
3. *Siddur Beit Ya'akov*, quoted in *Encyclopedia Judaica*, volume 6, page 724.
4. Responsa, Rashba, quoted in Louis Jacobs, *Theology in the Responsa* (London, 1975), page 73.
5. Berachot 35a.
6. Max Kadushin, *The Rabbinic Mind* (New York, 1952), page 168, note 1.
7. Menachot 43b.
8. MT Berachot 1:3.
9. MT Berachot 1:4.
10. Berachot 33a.
11. Berachot 40b.
12. Berachot 40b.
13. Tosafot, Berachot 40b, s.v. *amar Abayei*.
14. MT Berachot 11:16.
15. Tosafot, Ta'anit 28b, s.v. *amar shema mineh*.
16. Pesachim 7b.
17. See discussion in Tosafot, Pesachim 7b, s.v. *al ha-tevila*. The convert does not become a Jew until after immersion. The benediction is not appropriate until that time.
18. Tosafot, Sukka 39a, s.v. *over*.
19. *Encyclopedia Talmudit* (Jerusalem, 1952), volume 4, page 529, and note 167. Our custom differs. See Orach Chayim 263:5, Rema.
20. [19], volume 4, page 523.
21. Rashba, Responsa, No. 18; Ketubot 40a.
22. That is one reason given for omitting a blessing "Who sanctified us in His commandments" over recitation of the *Shema*. One may not be able to recite it with necessary *kavana*.
23. Chatam Sofer on Orach Chayim 54; [6], page 174, note 31.
24. Kadushin [6]; Torah Temima on Exod. 24:30.
25. Jacobs [4], pages 41-42.

26. Sukka 38b; Berachot 45b,53b. Judaism permits one person, under certain circumstances, to recite a benediction on behalf of another, to assist him in fulfilling a *mitzva*, based on the maxim that "all Jews are responsible for one another." Sanhedrin 27b; Shevu'ot 39a; Orach Chayim 167:19, Mishna Berura, note 92.
27. Shabbat 23a.
28. Kadushin [6], page 267.
29. Jacobs [4], page 20.
30. M. Yoma 6:2.
31. Even Shoshan, *Hebrew Dictionary*, Ridgefield edition (Jerusalem, 1980), volume 1, page 108.
32. Orach Chayim 124:6.
33. MT Berachot 1:13.
34. Sukka 51a.
35. Berachot 45a.
36. Pool PB, page 51.
37. Pool PB, page 68.
38. Pool PB, page 438; also after *Hallel*, page 352.
39. Hertz PB, pages 972-973.

## Notes to Chapter 13: Kaddish

1. Hertz PB, pages 106-107,186.
2. Hertz PB, pages 206-207,298.
3. Hertz PB, pages 236-239.
4. Hertz PB, pages 212-213.
5. Mishna Berura states that since the first two words are based on Ezekiel, the words should be pronounced as Hebrew, *Yitgadel ve-yitkadesh*, and not as Aramaic as is popularly done (comment on Orach Chayim 56:1, note 2).
6. Cf. *Sifre* to Deut. 32:3, which discusses responses to mention of God's Name.
7. David de Sola Pool, *The Kaddish* (New York, 1929), page 45.
8. [7], page 51.
9. Orach Chayim 56:1, Rema.
10. Birnbaum PB, page 116.
11. Hertz PB, pages 500-501.
12. [7], pages 76,77.
13. [7], page 71.
14. [7], page 71.
15. M Uketzin 3:12.
16. Soferim 10:7,16:12.
17. "And a Redeemer shall come to Zion." Hertz PB, pages 202-203; Sota 49a.
18. Berachot 3a; also Tosafot there s.v. *ve-onim*.
19. Proverbs Rabba on chapter 14, verse 28.
20. [7], page 9.
21. [7], pages 50-51.
22. Shabbat 119b.
23. Kalla Rabbati 2:9, page 52a. The legend originated in Seder Eliyahu Zuta. Versions of it are set forth in the *Jewish Encyclopedia* (1916 edition), volume 7, pages 401-402, entry *Kaddish*, and Elie Munk, *World of Prayer*, English translation (New York, 1953), volume 1, page 190.
24. Menorat ha-Ma'or dates to the 14th century. The legend is found in Ner Alef, Kelal Alef, part II.
25. [7], pages 102ff.
26. Sanhedrin 104a.
27. Berachot 21b; Megila 23b.
28. Orach Chayim 56.
29. [7], page 77, Yoma 53a-b.
30. M Eduyot 2:10; Rosh ha-Shana 17a.
31. Yoreh De'a 376:4, Rema; Munk [23], volume 1, page 191.
32. [18].

## Notes to Chapter 14: Torah Service

1. Megila 29b.
2. Mechilta, Lauterbach edition, volume 2, pages 89-90.
3. Bava Kama 82a.
4. MT Tefila, 12:1.
5. [3].
6. [3], s.v. *kedei shelo*.
7. Hertz PB, pages 188-189.
8. Avram Kampf, *Contemporary Synagogue Art* (Philadelphia, 1966), page 142; Uri Kaploun, editor, *The Synagogue*, JPS Popular Judaica Library (Philadelphia, 1973), page 103; M Ta'anit 2:1.
9. Shemot, portion *Va-Yakhel*; Soncino edition, volume IV, page 199.
10. [7], pages 474-475.
11. [7], pages 188-189.
12. [7], pages 480-481.
13. [7], pages 476-480.
14. [7], pages 190-191,484-485.
15. *ODM*, page 374.
16. MT Tefila 12:16; M Megila 3:1.
17. Megila 22b.
18. Megila 22a, Rashi on the Mishna.
19. Tosafot, Megila 23a, s.v. *keivan de-mishum*.
20. Megila 23a and Rashi, s.v. *mi-penei kavod*.
21. M Gitin 5:8.
22. Gitin 60a; *ODM*, page 374.
23. Megila 23a. Aaron H. Blumenthal, "An Aliyah for Women," Rabbinical Assembly, *Proceedings*, 1955, volume 19, pages 168-181; Sanders S. Tofield, "Women's Place in the Rites of the Synagogue," *op. cit.*, pages 182-190.
24. *ODM*, page 375.
25. [7], page 472.
26. MT Tefila 12:10.
27. *ODM*, page 375.
28. M Megila 4:4; Soferim 11:1.
29. Orach Chayim 137. Tosafot, Megila 21b, s.v. *ein pochatin*.
30. Megila 21b.
31. Megila 32a; Orach Chayim 139:4, and commentary, Mishna Berura, 139:11; Soferim 13:8.
32. MT Tefila 12:23.
33. Soferim 14:14. Orach Chayim 134:2, Mishna Berura, paragraph 8.
34. Megila 32a.

35. [7], pages 488-493.
36. [7], pages 490-491.
37. [7], pages 992-993.
38. [7], pages 486-487.
39. Berachot 54b.
40. Orach Chayim 219:3.
41. MT Berachot 10:8.
42. [7], pages 486-487.

# SELECTED BIBLIOGRAPHY

Abrahams, Israel. *Companion to the Authorised Daily Prayerbook*, new revised edition (New York, 1966).

_____. "Some Rabbinic Ideas on Prayer," in *Studies in Pharisaism and the Gospels*, 2nd series (Cambridge, 1924).

Albo, Joseph. *Sefer ha-Ikkarim (Book of Principles)*, translated by Isaac Husik (Philadelphia, 1946), volume IV.

Casper, Bernard M. *Talks on Jewish Prayer* (London, 1962).

Derovan, David. *Prayer: A Study Guide to the Philosophy and Meaning of Tefillah* (New York, 1970).

Eisenstein, J.D. *Otzar Dinim u-Minhagim (A Digest of Jewish Laws and Customs)* (New York, 1938).

Epstein, Isidore. *Judaism* (London, 1949).

Even-Shoshan, Avraham. *Milon Chadash*, Ridgefield edition, (Jerusalem, 1980).

Halevi, Judah. *The Kuzari*, translated by Hartwig Hirschfeld (New York, 1978).

Hertz, Joseph H. *Authorised Daily Prayer Book*, revised edition (New York, 1965).

Heschel, Abraham J. *The Insecurity of Freedom* (Philadelphia, 1956).

_____. *Man is Not Alone* (Philadelphia, 1951).

_____. *Man's Quest for God* (New York, 1954).

Hirsch, Samson Raphael. *Nineteen Letters of Ben Uziel*, translated by Bernard Drachman (New York, 1942).

_____. *Horeb*, translated by I. Grunfeld, (London, 1962).

Hurvitz, Simon. *The Responsa of Solomon Luria* (New York, 1938).

Jacobs, Louis. *Jewish Prayer* (London, 1962).

_____. *Hasidic Prayer (New York, 1975)*.

_____. *Theology in the Responsa* (London, 1975).

Jacobson, B.S. *The Weekday Siddur*, translated by Leonard Oschry, second edition (Tel Aviv, 1978).

_____. *Meditations on the Siddur*, translated by Leonard Oschry, (Tel Aviv, 1978).

Kadushin, Max. *Worship and Ethics* (Evanston, Ill., 1964).

_____. *The Rabbinic Mind* (New York, 1952).

Kagan, Israel Meir ha-Kohen. *Mishna Berura* (Commentary on *Shulchan Aruch*, Orach Chayim) (Jerusalem, 1970).

Karo, Joseph. *Shulchan Aruch (The Prepared Table)*, a code of Jewish law, in four parts. The part most frequently cited here is Orach Chayim, which deals with laws of daily observance, Sabbaths, and holidays.

Kaufmann, Yehezkel. *The Religion of Israel*, translated and abridged by Moshe Greenberg (Chicago, 1960).

Klein, Isaac. *Guide to Jewish Religious Practice* (New York, 1979).

Kon, Abraham Israel. *Prayer* (London, 1971).

Maimonides, Moses. *Guide for the Perplexed*, translated by M. Friedlander, second edition (New York, 1956).

_____. *Mishneh Torah*, also known as *Yad ha-Chazaka* (Jerusalem, 1969).

_____. *Rambam la-Am*, edited with commentary by Samuel T. Rubenstein (Tel Aviv, 1949).

*Mekilta de-Rabbi Ishmael*, translated by Jacob Z. Lauterbach, paperback edition (Philadelphia, 1976).

*Midrash Rabbah*, Soncino translation, edited by H. Freedman and M. Simon (London, 1951).

Milgrom, Abraham. *Jewish Worship* (Philadelphia, 1971).

Moore, George Foot. *Judaism in the First Centuries of the Christian Era*, Schocken paperback edition (New York, 1971).

Munk, Elie. *World of Prayer*, translated by Henry Biberfeld and Leonard Oschry (New York, 1953).

Pool, David de Sola. *The Kaddish* (New York, 1929).

*Talmud* (Babylonian), Hebrew–English edition, Soncino Press (London, 1960).

*Talmud* (Jerusalem), Hebrew, following Krotoshin edition, 1866 (Jerusalem, 5729).

# INDEX

ABRAHAM, 31, 44, 75
  source of blessing, 76
  virtues of forefathers, 43, 75
ABRAHAMS, Israel, 16, 62
ABUDRAHAM, Rabbi David, 60, 89
ADON OLAM, 40, 41
AFFIRMATION OF FAITH, 4, 5, 40-41
AFTERNOON SERVICE, see MINCHA
AHAVA RABBA benediction, 54, 57-58, 101, 111, 124
AHAVAT OLAM benediction, 57, 69
AKIBA, Rabbi, 54, 98, 133-134
AL HA-NISIM prayer, 92-93
ALBO, Joseph, 6-8, 167
ALIYA, 139
AMEN
  meaning, 127-128
  when recited, 41, 69, 88, 90, 100, 130, 132, 133
AMIDA (see also SHEMONEH ESREH)
  generally, 73-94
  Avot benediction, 27
  community prayer, 34, 35
  Jerusalem, recited facing, 31
  kavana, 24, 25, 27
  language, 20
  makeup prayers, 34
  names of, 73
  nineteen benedictions on weekdays, 73
  phrasing in plural, 34, 78
  position during, 95, 96, 97
  preliminary verses, 74-75
  Priestly Benediction, 86, 89-90
  private prayers, 19, 34, 78, 93
  rain prayers, 91-92
  repetition of, 88-90
  Shalom Rav, 86
  Sim Shalom, 86-87
  structure of, 74, 75-87
  supplication prayers, 74, 78-84
  thanksgiving (Modim) prayer, 84-87
  three sections of, 74
  time for recitation of, 32-33, 68
  Ya'aleh ve-Yavo (new moon and festival) prayer, 92

ANENU prayer on fast days, 93
ARAMAIC, use in prayers,
  language of Kaddish, 135
  translation of Torah reading, 140
ARVIT, see MA'ARIV
ASHREI prayer, 46, 47, 48, 71, 102, 103
  composition of, 49-50
  recited three times daily, 49
AVOT (forefathers) benediction, 75

BARECHU, 53-54, 134
  call to worship, 53
  minyan required, 53
  phraseology, 53-54
BARUCH ADONAI LE-OLAM
  benediction, 71-72
  substitute for Amida, 71
BARUCH SHE-AMAR prayer, 49, 52, 95, 101, 102
  commences Pesukei de-Zimra, 47
  complete benediction, 47
  format, 47-48
BARUCH SHEM KEVOD, 62, 63, 130
BENEDICTION, see BERACHA
BERACHA, 1, 76, 122-128
  categories of, 123
  format of, 123-125
  mention of God's Kingship, 97, 124-125
  occasions of, 123, 126
  over custom, 118, 125
  philosophical problems, 122-123
  precedes act, 123, 125-126, 167
  recitation of Amen, 127-128
  recited by another, 127
  vain blessing, 40, 44, 126, 167

BERICH SHEMEH prayer, 138
BOWING IN PRAYER, 53, 75, 85, 97, 134
BREAST-BEATING, at confession, 103, 163

CANTOR, see CHAZAN
CHANUKA, 92-93, 127, 136, 139
CHAZAN
  origin of, 22-23, 149
  qualifications of, 23, 149
  Sheliach Tzibur, 23, 88
CHET (sin), 79
CONFESSION OF SINS, 1, 79
CONGREGATIONAL WORSHIP
  preference for, 34-37
  public prayer, 35-36, 152
  quorum or minyan during, 33, 35-37
COVERING THE HEAD, see HEADCOVERING

DRESS for prayer
  Amida, 104
  headcovering, 105-108
  kittel, 116
  leather shoes, 115
  sash (gartel), 115
  Shema, 104
DUCHEN, 89

EDA, see MINYAN
EIGHTEEN BENEDICTIONS, see SHEMONEH ESREH
ELOHAI NESHAMA prayer, 40
ELUL, 119
EMDEN, Rabbi Jacob, 10, 122
EMET VE-EMUNA benediction, 70
EMET VE-YATZIV benediction, 5, 54, 55, 66-67, 70
  Ge'ula prayer joined to Amida, 67, 68-69
ETROG, 26, 116-118

# INDEX

EVENING SERVICE, see MA'ARIV
EZRA, 137

FRINGES, see TZITZIT

GAON OF WILNA, 27-28, 72, 84
GARTEL (sash), 115
GESTURES in prayer
 beating the heart, 103
 bowing (and bending the knees) 53, 97, 134
 covering eyes, 102-103
 kissing ritual objects, 101-102, 164
 opening the hand, 103
 rising on toes, 99-100
 steps forward and back, 97, 98, 134-135
 swaying, 98-99
GE'ULA (redemption) prayer joined to Amida, 67-69, 71
GEVUROT (strengths) benediction, 75
GRADE, Chaim, The Yeshiva, 19

HAFTARA, 138, 139, 142
HALEVI, Judah, xi, 2-3, 28, 30, 35, 54, 55, 67, 77, 99
HALLEL, 46, 50, 115, 118
HANNAH, 100
HASHKIVENU benediction, 70, 71, 72
HAT, see HEADCOVERING
HAVDALA, 92, 120-121
HAVINENU prayer, 94
HEADCOVERING
 definition, 107
 kippa, 102, 105
 reasons for, 105-107
 yarmulka, 102, 108
HEALING benediction, 80
HERTZ, Joseph H., Chief Rabbi, 5, 36, 45

HESCHEL, Rabbi Abraham J., 3, 9, 10, 11, 12, 19
HEZEKIAH, King, 30
HIRSCH, Rabbi Samson Raphael, 4, 5, 8, 9, 79, 122

ISAAC, 14, 75

JACOB, 14, 62, 75
JERUSALEM, 92
 benediction, 83
 facing in prayer, 31

KADDISH, generally, 129-135
 development of, 132-134
 language of, 135
 minyan required for, 37, 134
 mourner's prayer, 129, 130, 132-135
 recited standing, 95, 134
 steps forward and back at the end of, 97, 134-135
KADDISH, Half, 48, 52, 71, 72, 129, 130-131, 139, 141, 142
KADDISH, Mourner's, 129, 130, 131
KADDISH, Rabbinic (de-Rabbanan) 45, 129, 131
KADDISH SHALEM (Reader's Kaddish), 129, 131
KAVANA
 definitions of, 25, 27
 rabbinic debate over, 25
 in recitation of Amida, 27
 in recitation of Shema, 25, 27, 58
 requirement in prayer, 25, 27-28
KEDUSHA DA-AMIDA, 56, 57, 77-78, 88, 89, 95, 96, 99
 minyan required, 37, 56, 77, 89
KEDUSHA DE-SIDRA (U-Va le-Tziyon) 56, 77, 132

KEDUSHA DE-YOTZER, 56-57, 77, 89
KITTEL, 116
KNEELING, 96, 97
KOOK, Abraham Isaac, Chief Rabbi, 146, 151

LEVITES, 53, 135, 139-140
LULAV, 26, 116-118
LURIA, Rabbi Isaac, 50, 103
LURIA, Rabbi Solomon, 105, 163

MA TOVU prayer, 40
MA'ARIV, 14
  time period for, 33
MAFTIR, 139, 140, 141
MAIMONIDES, Moses, 2, 4, 13, 25, 26, 27, 30, 56, 62, 74, 101, 103, 104, 109, 123, 151, 166
MATZA, 25, 26
MEN OF THE GREAT ASSEMBLY, xi, 14, 18, 123
MESSIAH, 83, 130
MINCHA, 14
  Mincha Gedola, 33
  Pelag Mincha, 33
  time period for, 32-33
MINYAN, 30, 33
  definition of, 36-37, 56
  when required, 36-37, 53, 77, 89, 134, 136, 152
MODIM, prayer, 85-86, 89, 97
MODIM DE-RABBANAN prayer, 89, 97
MORNING BENEDICTIONS, see PRELIMINARY BLESSINGS
MOSES, 17, 51, 74, 76, 137
MOURNERS' PRAYER, see KADDISH
MUSAF, 14, 32, 77, 86, 89, 92

MUSIC, 21-23
  cantor (chazan) 22-23
  instruments, use of, 23
  nusach, 22

NACHMANIDES, Moses (Ramban) 13, 59, 64
NETILAT YADAYIM, 38-39
NEW MOON, 92, 115, 125, 136, 139
NUSACH, 22

OSEH SHALOM verse, 97, 131-132, 134

PESUKEI DE-ZIMRA, 46-52, 124
  Ashrei, 48, 49-50
  Baruch she-Amar, 47, 124
  contents, 48-52
  Hallelujah Psalms, 48, 50
  origin and purpose of, 46-47
  Psalm of Thanksgiving, 48-49
  Song of Moses, 48, 51-52
  Yishtabach, 47, 48, 51, 52
PHYLACTERIES, see TEFILIN
POOL, Rabbi David de Sola, 42, 130, 131, 132, 134
POSITION IN PRAYER, generally, 95-100
  bowing (and bending the knees) 53, 97, 134
  falling on the face, 95, 96
  feet together, 96, 110
  kneeling restricted, 96, 97
  rising on toes, 99-100
  sitting, 95, 96
  standing, 95, 96
  steps forward and back, 97, 98, 134-135

# INDEX

PRAYER
  answering of, 5, 7, 8
  categories of, 1
  communication with God during, 1, 2, 3, 4
  congregational and individual prayer, 34-37
  early forms of, 1-2
  formulas, 18-19
  frame of mind during, 24-25
  importance to the Jew, 2-3
  influencing God, 1, 2, 6
  influencing man, 1, 2, 3, 4, 6-7, 8
  kavana (intent) during, 24-25
  language of, 19-21
  length of, 17-18
  in low place, 30
  as mitzva, 2, 13
  as petition, 5, 6, 7-9
  philosophy of, 1-12
  place of, 29-31
  as praise and blessing, 1, 10
  preparation for, 24-25
  public prayer, 35-36
  purpose of, 2, 4, 9
  questionable concepts, 11-12
  spontaneity of, 16, 19
  time of, 31-33
  vain prayers, 6, 40, 44, 126, 167
PRAYER, PLACE OF, 29-31
  clean, 30
  facing Jerusalem, 30-31
  facing wall, 30
  fixed place, 31
  low, 30
  room with windows, 30-31
PRAYER SERVICES, 14-16
  established by Patriarchs, 14
  Ma'ariv, evening, 14, 33
  Mincha, afternoon, 14, 32-33
  Musaf, additional, 14, 32
  Shacharit, morning, 14, 32, 86, 89
  substitute for sacrifices, 14-16, 44
  three principal services, 15-16
PRAYER SHAWL, see TALIT
PRAYER, TIME OF
  computing hours, 31-32
  linked to sacrifices, 31-33
  specific prayers, 32-33
PRELIMINARY BLESSINGS, 38-45
  Elohai Neshama, 40
  morning benedictions, 41
  sacrifical selections, 44-45
  Shema, abbreviated, 43-44
  Torah study benedictions, 39-40, 44
  washing the hands, 38-39
PRIESTLY BENEDICTION, 86, 89-90, 102
PRIESTS (Kohanim) 86, 89-90, 102, 106, 140
PURIM, 92-93, 139, 140

RAIN PRAYERS, 77, 91-92
RAM'S HORN, see SHOFAR
REDEMPTION benedictions, 68, 80, 130
REPENTANCE benediction, 79
RESURRECTION OF THE DEAD, 76, 77
RETZEH, 84, 90
ROSH CHODESH, see NEW MOON

SACRIFICES, 44-45, 84, 92
SELICHA (forgiveness) benediction, 79
SHA'OT ZEMANIYOT (seasonal hours), 31-32
SHALOM RAV, 86

SHEMA, BENEDICTIONS OF, 54-58, 66-67, 155
  evening, 69-72
  morning, 54, 55-58, 66-67
SHEMA, READING OF, 44, 58-66
  affirmation of faith, 63
  allusion to Ten Commandments, 64-66
  Baruch Shem Kevod, 62-63
  benedictions, 54-58, 66-72, 124, 126
  contents, 63-64
  customs associated with first verse, 60-61, 101, 102, 110
  declaration of God's Unity, 59, 60, 102-103
  El Melech Ne'eman, 61
  kavana required, 25, 27, 58, 60
  meaning of first verse, 59-60
  position during, 96
  recited in any language, 19-20, 60
  time of, 31, 32, 33
  Va-yomer, included at night, 70
SHEMONEH ESREH (see also AMIDA)
  eighteen benedictions originally, 73
  format, 74
  intermediate blessings on weekdays, 74, 78-84
  minim (sectarians) 73-74, 81-82, 83
  name not changed, 73-74
  name of weekday prayer, 73
  nineteenth benediction added, 73-74, 81-82, 83
  private prayers added, 93
  rain prayers, 91-92
  shortened version, 94
  steps forward and back, 74-75, 87-88

SHOFAR, 25, 98, 118-120, 165
SIDROT (weekly Torah portions), 136
SIM SHALOM, 86, 87
SWAYING (shoklen) in prayer, 98-99

TALIT, 25, 95, 102, 107, 108-112, 141
  derivation of word, 112
  donned before tefilin, 110-111
  for single men, 108
  on Tish'a be-Av, 111
  for women, 111
TEFILA, see AMIDA
TEFILIN, 26, 95, 102, 110, 111, 112-115
  contents of, 113
  for lefthanded person, 113
  Rashi, Rabbenu Tam, 113, 114
  when not worn, 112-113
TEN COMMANDMENTS, 64-66, 137
TEN DAYS OF PENITENCE, 90-91, 131
TESHUVA, see REPENTANCE
THANKSGIVING
  benediction in Amida, 85-86
  benediction when called to Torah, 143
  Psalm of, 48-49, 95
THIRTEEN ARTICLES OF FAITH, of Maimonides, 41
TISH'A BE-AV, 93, 111, 115
TORAH
  benedictions on reading, 140-141
  benedictions on study, 39-40, 44
  reader, 140
  reading in synagogue, 136-143
  number called to, 139
  number of verses read, 140

# INDEX

TZEDAKA (charity), 103
TZITZIT, 63, 64, 70, 101, 108-112

U-VA LE-TZIYON GO'EL prayer, 56, 77, 114, 132
U-VE-NUCHO YOMAR, 142
UNITY OF GOD declaration, 101, 102-103

VA-YEHI BI-NESOA, 137-138
VOICE, modulation of, in prayer, 100-101

WASHING OF HANDS, 38-39

WOMEN, 42-43
 called to Torah, 140
 talit, worn by, 111

YA'ALEH VE-YAVO prayer, 92
YARMULKA (see also HEAD-COVERING), 102, 108
YIGDAL, 5, 40, 41
YISHTABACH, 47, 48, 51, 52, 95, 124, 128
YOTZER OR benediction, 54, 55-57, 66, 124

ZECHUT AVOT (merits of forefathers) 43, 75

181

# GUIDES TO JEWISH FAMILY LIVING

*The Five Scrolls*
Five of the most beloved books of the Bible in an edition of stunning beauty and power. Fully illustrated with 37 new Leonard Baskin watercolors.
Congregational edition $15.00
Deluxe Art Edition $60.00
Limited Edition $675.00

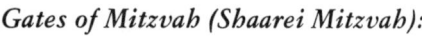

*Gates of Mitzvah (Shaarei Mitzvah):*
*A Guide to the Jewish Life Cycle*
Birth, childhood, education, marriage, the Jewish home, death and mourning. Illustrated $7.95

*Gates of the Seasons (Shaarei Mo-Eid):*
*A Guide to the Jewish Year*
Observing and understanding the sacred days that are the cycle of the Jewish Year. Illustrated $9.95

*Shabbat Manual*
Celebrating Shabbat in the spirit of modern times.
Hardcover $5.95

*A Passover Haggadah*
The perfect companion guide to your Passover celebration. Features complete home service, 24 brilliant Leonard Baskin illustrations, non-sexist language and festival songs.
Softcover $7.50   Deluxe Art Edition $27.50
Seder Set (1 Deluxe Art edition and 10 softcover copies) $79.00

Available at Sisterhood Judaica shops, local Jewish bookstores or directly from the CCAR.

**Central Conference of American Rabbis**
**21 East 40th Street, New York, NY 10016**

*Also from Alpha Publishing:*

# WEDDINGS
## A Complete Guide to All Religious and Interfaith Marriage Services

by
*Abraham J. Klausner*

Everything you always wanted to know about weddings: Symbols, Customs, Ceremonies, Time and Place, Arrangements, and much more.

Complete texts for all traditional, contemporary, and innovative marriage services: Protestant, Catholic, Jewish, Interfaith, Episcopal, Presbyterian, Methodist, Unitarian, Muslim, and many more.

An ideal reference tool for persons who perform marriage services and for those about to be married.

ISBN 0-933771-00-2. Soft cover.

Order now from:

**Alpha Publishing Company**
a division of
Special Edition, Inc.
3497 East Livingston Avenue
Columbus, Ohio 43227
(614) 231-4088